Navigating the Clickety-Clack

NAVIGATING THE CLICKETY-CLACK

How to Live a Peace-Filled Life in a Seemingly Toxic World

Volume 2

Featuring:
International Bestselling Authors
Marie Diamond, Adam Markel, and Joe Vitale

Also Featuring:
Contributing Authors — Phyllis Marlene Benstein, Kathy Bradley, Katherine
Brooke-MacKenzie, Cindy Costley, Dario Cucci, Brian Evans, Naomi
Gillespie, Deanna Hansen, Brigitte Keane, Lidia Kuleshnyk,
Gwen Lepard, Jason Daveon Mitchell, Cassie Schwind, Jennifer Sprague,
Linda Tan, Lisa Warner, and Leslie Warren

BEYOND
BELIEF
—PUBLISHING—
YOU HOLD THE FUTURE IN YOUR HANDS

Rev. Michael Beckwith and Fletch Rainey

This book is dedicated to our dear friend and spiritual mentor, Fletch Rainey. RIP, dear Fletch. May your teachings about the Clickety-Clack live on and serve humanity for many years to come.

Praise for *Navigating the Clickety-Clack Volume 2*

"This book is an absolute game changer. Turned my world upside down in the best possible way."

~Serrin Mccallum

"Each person in this book can teach you something valuable to UNLOCK your best life and future. You are worthy of your best life!"

~Darius M. Barazandeh,
You Wealth Revolution Founder and Creator

"More than ever before in our lives, we need hope, to feel understood, and be given practical resources that enable us to find peace within ourselves, regardless of what is going on in the outside world. Each page of this book carries with it ageless wisdom and truth and the encouragement that comes from an invisible comforting arm around your shoulders."

~Peter Steedman, Internationally renowned Psychic Surgeon,
Intuitive Therapist, Medium, and Soul Healer

"Difficult times affect us all. How refreshing it is to learn the different ways in which these authors view and deal with their respective challenges. You will simply feel uplifted after reading this book."

~Michelle Eddahar,
Entrepreneur and Business Networking Goddess

"*Navigating the Clickety-Clack* is filled with suggestions and experiences that help you navigate your erratic reactions to the outside stimulus of fear-based change that we are now asked to create as humanity shifts into a new era."

~Joan Walker, Ascension Facilitator and Channel

"So many pearls of wisdom in this book! *Navigating the Clickety-Clack* is a must-read for anyone seeking to create a happier, healthier, more peaceful life."

~Melissa Deally, Integrative Health Practitioner, Registered Health Coach, and Creator of Your Guided Health Journey

"When you can turn down the volume on the Clickety-Clack, you can turn up the volume on your inner super-hero and rise above the noise to create the life of your dreams. Let these stories help inspire the superhero in you."

~Damian Nordmann, Business Coach, Mindset Coach, Mentor to Superheroes

"This book is filled with wisdom, guidance, inspiration, and insights that are guaranteed to help anyone who is trying to *Navigate the Clickety-Clack*."

~Tyson Sharpe, Emotional Fitness Coach, Creator of The Serving Circle for Heart-Centered CEO Collaboration

"*Navigating the Clickety-Clack* is uplifting, inspiring, and timely. A *must-read* to encourage confidence, calm, and courage."

~Barbara Gallagher, President, Luxury Outerwear/Spiritual Silks

"Gwen Lepard provides an insightful tool for changing how you are feeling in moments of stress. I recommend this read for anyone who gets bogged down by the day-to-day."

~Eiji "A.G." Morishita, Founder of Movement Makers

"Navigating the Clickety-Clack is a must-read for anyone who wants to turn back the clock of time and find inner fulfillment."
~Tammy and Barry Gibson, Authors, Golf Success Coaches, founders of Hole In One Success

"This is a good book for you if you are done living a life of frustration and anger and you want a way to build a life filled with peace, joy, and freedom."
~Naomi Fox, Artist

"Navigating the Clickety-Clack, Volume 2 is a must-read for anyone who has stress and frustration in their life (everyone!?) and is ready to 'click into a new gear,' especially one that includes emotional and spiritual well-being. Grab a copy for yourself and get one for your best friend."
~Ursula Mentjes, CEO and Founder of Sales Coach Now

"This is definitely something that, as a business owner, is one of the hardest things to navigate—keeping the faith during those moments of Clickety-Clack. Love it."
~Alex Brzozowski, Professional Organizer

"I like the practical and real-life application given in this book that can lead to great results."
~Abigail Hunter

"I highly suggest reading this book for help with navigating the unpredictable seas of life. Wonderful guidance for finding greater peace and calm, as well as ways of acquiring powerful tools for personal growth and evolution."
~Andrea Sperling, College Professor/Singer-Songwriter

"Are people around you freaking out, coming unglued, being judgmental, hateful, or angry? *Navigating the Clickety-Clack* will help you learn to keep your center and stay peaceful."

~Heather Meglasson, Impact Artist

"*Navigating the Clickety-Clack* is a must-read for anyone who wants peace and calm in their life."

~Melaney Swan, Public Service Worker

"Contributing author Gwen Lepard provides an insightful tool for changing how you are feeling in the moment of stress. I recommend this read."

~Heike Mannix, Professional Organizer

"*Navigating the Clickety-Clack* gives real-world guidance in handling the negative and enforcing the positive. If you're looking for joy and change for the better, this is the book for you."

~Jeihan Cluney, Lab Technician

"*How to Live a Peace-Filled Life in a Seemingly Toxic World* is easy when you take the advice of these best-selling and featured authors."

~Michelle Morrigan, Founder of Goddess Rising

"*Navigating the Clickety-Clack* takes [what] may be a vague concept in our lives that we go through with a certain amount of numbness and brings practicality to that very real space in our lives. It certainly deserves attention so it can be properly dismantled."

~Lauri Hunter

Contents

Acknowledgments 13

Introduction 15

Phyllis Marlene Benstein 19

Kathy Bradley 25

Katherine Brooke-MacKenzie 33

Cindy Costley 39

Dario Cucci 45

Marie Diamond 51

Brian Evans 55

Naomi Gillespie 63

Deanna Hansen 69

Brigitte Keane 77

Lidia Kuleshnyk 83

Gwen Lepard 91

Adam Markel 97

Jason Daveon Mitchell 105

Cassie Schwind 111

Jennifer Sprague 117

Linda Tan 125

Joe Vitale 131

Lisa Warner 137

Leslie Warren 145

Conclusion 151

About the Publisher 153

Acknowledgments

It is with deep appreciation that I thank all the authors who said YES to participating in this powerful project.

Thanks to Marie Diamond, Adam Markel, and Joe Vitale for being such great mentors and for always saying yes. Your support over the years has been instrumental in our success as authors and publishers.

Thank you to our incredible team who brought this book forward to completion and to the world one step at a time: Karen Burton, Heather Taylor, Bethany Knowles, Autumn Carlton, MaryDes, Rudy Milanovich, Viki Winterton, Pam Murphy, and Mark Steven Pooler.

Thank you to all the teachers, speakers, and thought leaders who provided the tips, tools, and workshops that taught the master teachers in this book how to stay peaceful, even during the Clickety-Clack of everyday life.

Keith Leon S.

Introduction

Hello. My name is Keith Leon S., owner of Beyond Belief Publishing, and I want to welcome you to our book, designed to help you Navigate the Clickety-Clack. As we begin this journey together, you may not yet understand the title, but I am confident you navigate this troubling place from time to time. We all do.

Back in 2005, my wife, Maura, and I met a man named Fletch Rainey at the Agape International Center of Truth in California. We became good friends with Fletch. Eventually he created a group called "The Spiritual Posse" and became one of our spiritual mentors. We would reach out to him when we were freaking out about money, business challenges, fears, or when we were in flux, not knowing what to do next.

One time when we called him with one of our issues, he said, "Relax, you are just in the Clickety-Clack."

We asked, "What is the Clickety-Clack?"

Fletch said, "Remember when you had a ten-speed bicycle, and you changed from one gear to another? There is that moment when the chain is jumping from one gear to the next gear, but it has not clicked in yet. What sound does it make? *Clickety-clack . . . clickety-clack.* You have faith it will catch eventually, so you keep peddling the bike. Your faith pays off because it eventually catches, and when it does, you are off into an even better gear. That is where you are right now—you are in the Clickety-Clack. Have faith and know that things will kick into the next gear soon enough. Trust, and know that all is well."

His reply has stayed with us, and to this day, when Maura and I are experiencing worry or not knowing what to do next, one of us will look at the other and say "Clickety-Clack." Other times I have experienced the Clickety-Clack are when others around me are freaking out, coming unglued, and being judgmental, hateful, or angry toward me.

In a world filled with so much anger, resentment, judgment, hate, shame, and finger-pointing, how is one supposed to stay peaceful?

Over the years, I have developed tools to remain calm and peaceful in these times. People have asked me how I am able to do this. The answer is multi-layered, and it has taken me years to arrive at this point.

Here are some practices that have helped me over the years:

- Experiential growth workshops
- *The Work* of Byron Katie
- Prayer and meditation
- Teachings from the mystics
- Minding my thoughts and language

In the spring of 2020, the COVID-19 pandemic kept us all in our homes. This was a time of inner reflection for me. I took time to go within and look for answers to the question: *What's next for me?* I had visions of our dear friend Fletch and his teaching us about the Clickety-Clack. I thought: *If ever there were a time to stay calm and peaceful, it's now.*

With so much seemingly toxic information, news, and energy around us, wouldn't now be a great time to gain some tools for neutrality? I thought to myself: *I know people who are living these principles every day. I am friends with people who are able to stay peaceful, even now.* This thought led me to reach out to three dear friends and mentors, Bob Proctor, Jack Canfield, and Christy Whitman. I shared the title and subtitle with them, and they said they would love to participate in the book.

Next, I made a short list of other friends who were walking and talking demonstrations of staying peaceful when others could not. I contacted these friends and asked them if they would like to participate. At the end of each call, I asked each friend, "Do you know someone who is living a peace-filled life in a seemingly toxic world?" The people they recommended appeared in the first Clickety-Clack book. Every person in this book lives this principle. For Volume 2, I did the same process. First, I called Marie Diamond, Joe Vitale, and Adam Markel. Then, I repeated the process mentioned above to find the additional authors.

Each person in this book is living what they share and teach you!

I suggest taking your time to read this book. Read one story at a time, then stop and meditate on what was shared. Take notes, write in a journal, and decide if there is a next step you would like to take, such as researching teachers, programs, or seminars recommended.

I have put together for you the finest group of people to share their Clickety-Clack stories, how they navigated out of the Clickety-Clack, and how they are able to stay peaceful inside, no matter what is happening outside. May you enjoy each and every word. May you be guided to next steps and ultimately discover what is called *the peace that passes all understanding.*

Phyllis Marlene Benstein

How has the Clickety-Clack shown up in your life?

The Clickety-Clack showed up in my life at a young age. I had allergies and sensitivities both to foods and my environment; different toxins made me sick. When I was five years old, I had anaphylactic shock and was rushed to the emergency room after eating smoked salmon.

The Clickety-Clack also showed up in my toxic marriage and in my toxic work environment when I worked as an electrical engineer. I thought I had it all. I thought I had a great marriage, a great house, a great job, and four beautiful kids. Then, it turned toxic. I had not married the right guy. I ended up in an emotionally abusive marriage.

I knew something needed to change. I knew all these things were making me sick, and the toxins were adding up in my system from all sides—from the continuing allergies and sensitivities to my relationships, both personally and professionally.

Another thing that set me up in the Clickety-Clack is that I grew up as a fine arts person—singing, dancing, and acting. My dream was to go to college and become an actress or a musician. My dad smashed that goal. He was a mathematician, and he strongly suggested I study engineering. So, that set me into the Clickety-Clack just as I emerged as an adult.

How did you navigate the Clickety-Clack?

I needed to do some self-inspection because it was a recurring pattern of these things making me sick. I really looked inside myself. I looked at what my core values were, what my core beliefs were, what my dreams were. What I was doing was not working, so, I embraced who I was from the inside.

I never gave up on my dreams and my hopes. I kept that hope alive. I empowered myself to evolve. I realized I never wanted to settle for less in my life or in my job—my life's work—than I knew I deserved. I always looked for best-in-class solutions.

I began on a path of personal development. I joined CEO Space, which broadened my horizons and helped me think bigger. This organization also brought me more business resources, higher level connections, and a better community.

I was introduced to a company called Monat Global that sells nontoxic, gluten-free, vegan products. These products helped me detox my physical self by changing what I was putting on and in my body. I pulled it all together with Brand Builders Club, as they have been helping me reframe everything and tie together all items related to detox.

All in all, I have been through an evolution. That is how I navigated things, by getting rid of the negativity because I know life is defined by the five people we hang around with most. I started peeling away the skin of the onion—what was not working for me, not in alignment with my ultimate dreams and goals.

Whatever was not in alignment had to go. I divorced my husband. I left my engineering job in 2011, never to look back, and have been an entrepreneur ever since. I helped myself heal, and it has been a process.

What tools do you recommend for staying peaceful in a seemingly toxic world?

There is a little bit of overlap between never settling for less and never giving up on dreams. I could have stayed in my marriage; I could have stayed in my engineering career, and I would have been miserable. I am a strong believer in introspection and personal development.

I learned to go inside myself. I learned to keep dreaming. I am a meditator and a manifestor. I was an RF microwave engineer, working with energy, and I now work with the energy within myself and my environment. I am always grounding myself. I am a tree hugger. I have raised my own awareness of self and also of what is possible.

Another tool I used was detoxing relationships. If you are in a relationship that is cutting you down—that is negative, that is not helping you be the best version of yourself—it is not worth it. In the career I have chosen, I educate people worldwide about the toxins in self-care products and their effects on your body.

One tool I learned along the way since I had aphylactic shock was to read labels. I read every single food label when I buy food in the grocery store. If it is processed or has certain ingredients in it, I put it down. I do not want to have another aphylactic shock event.

I took care of four beautiful kids as a single mom for about a dozen years. And so, I do my research. That is another tool. Never take anything for face value. The engineer in me knows I need to do research, and I need to make choices based on the evidence, based on the facts. Through the Monat Global opportunity, I have not only detoxed my skin, my hair, and my body, but I have helped others do the same as well.

I have helped others see where they are right now in their businesses. That is another skill I possess—helping people transform from employee or engineer to entrepreneur. I want people to have that bounce-back ability because I believe the biggest tool is the ability to reset. You need to reset if you are not where you want to be or not headed in the right direction.

Never give up on your dreams.

About the Author

Phyllis Marlene Benstein is an international speaker, bestselling author, a Legacy Founding Leader, Cadillac Earner, and an Independent Market Partner with Monat Global as well as a beauty influencer. She is published in the United States and England. Her background is in electrical engineering, and she serves as a role model for others to transition from corporate employment to entrepreneurship, experiencing a successful second career after age fifty.

Through speaking, workshops, coaching, and signature events, she educates the public and health and beauty professionals about toxins in hair and skincare products and their effects, while providing a complete line of toxin-free, vegan, gluten-free, cruelty-free, anti-aging products. She also provides a phenomenal financial opportunity for those who advocate clean-living lifestyle products and would like to be compensated for it.

Phyllis splits her time between Colorado and Florida with her husband Harry. She is the mother of two grown daughters and two grown sons. She is a Glamma to two beautiful granddaughters and two handsome grandsons, as well as a friend to so many she calls family.

If you relate to Phyllis's story or would like to learn more about the resources she recommends to become a great entrepreneur or the products she uses to detox her mind, body, and spirit, go to PhyllisMarlene.com. You can also contact her there to speak at your next event, seminar, or meeting. If you would love to explore the products and business opportunity of her International Monat Global team, go to Phyllis.myMonat.com.

Contact Info: phyllis@phyllismarlene.com or linkedin.com/in/phyllismarlenebenstein

Kathy Bradley

How has the Clickety-Clack shown up in your life?

I was an entrepreneur, financially successful for twenty-five years. I was really unhappy in my career. I felt irritated and anxious. I wondered: *What is this all about?* I seemingly had everything—a good job, a nice house, a beautiful marriage—and yet something was still missing. I was not happy.

Well, this unhappiness brought me to a turning point—a place of realization that my life was not what I originally thought it would be. And so, I asked myself: *What am I to do?* I was afraid, I felt stuck, and I was unsure of myself. I wondered what people would think of me if I shifted out of a financially rewarding career into working with the Angelic Realm, into working with people to help them find their true divine purpose.

And yet, there was a curiosity and a yearning that came with this.

How did you navigate the Clickety-Clack?

The first thing I did was breath work. That work brought me into the present moment, to my *I am* presence. When I am in that moment, in those three consecutive breaths, no thought is thought. This is where we connect with the void. When we are

25

in this place, we relax, we allow, and we open up to possibilities without needing anything.

We are often stressed, and when we are stressed, we often cut ourselves off from this internal guidance system, our GPS. I would connect with myself on a daily basis, and I would connect with my entourage, as I call them. I would ask my Higher Self, my Angels, my Guides: *What would you like to share with me in this Now moment?* And then, I would be quiet and listen. I take action where I am guided by this GPS, and I always express gratitude, knowing that the information I am offered is for my highest good.

The other thing I did is shifted my focus from outside—what I thought other people wanted me to do—and moved into a place of self-acceptance, self-appreciation, and self-realization. I stopped taking my cue from the outside world and what others would think. I connected with my Higher Self, which, I have learned, never leads me astray.

For the next step, I shifted my perspective from what I *did not* want to what I *did* want. So often we are caught up in what we do not want and focus on that, without even realizing we do it. Then, from this new space, I asked: *How may I serve?* That question moved me out of my ego and brought me into a place of following my heart, where I felt good and light and happy.

I also realized an important fact: being and acting in alignment with my calling provides everything I need.

I decided to transition slowly, in a part-time manner, into what I wanted to create, into this new place of offering people guidance, self-awareness, and empowering tools. I also set my energetic boundaries and my delineation point by using a tool called *The Rose*. It cleared my thoughts, my feelings, and my desires.

What tools do you recommend for staying peaceful in a seemingly toxic world?

First, practice the breath work: three consecutive circular breathes, where no thought is thought.

Then, awaken and nurture your internal guidance system. Ask your Higher Self, your Angels and Guides: *What do you want to share with me?* Be open and allow the information to pour through. Give yourself a few moments and jot down whatever comes to you, without editing and judging it. This is a process. Ask, then surrender—similar to writing a letter to someone. You do not dictate how it should be answered or what you expect. You surrender, then listen.

Finally, take action where guided and give gratitude. My greatest hope is for you to experience that *aha* and realize you are a powerful creator. You are divine. One of the best ways of doing this is by placing your attention on your intention. Our words are powerful, and when we state: *I am (fill in the blank)*, we are calling those words into reality. Every thought, feeling, and action holds energy.

We need to shift our perspective from limiting, lack-filled beliefs to positive, unlimited possibilities. One of the best ways to do this is with sacred geometry. I love working with the triangle.

For example, look at lack-filled, limiting beliefs that weigh you down, such as:

- *I doubt myself.*

- *I am frazzled.*
- *I am afraid.*
- *I am guilty.*
- *I am confused.*
- *I am unsure.*
- *I am stuck.*

Now, shift those limiting lack filled beliefs to positive ones, such as:

- *I am certain.*
- *I am confident.*
- *I am happy.*
- *I am at ease.*
- *I allow.*
- *I trust.*

Breathe those statements in and feel the difference in your environment, in your body, in your thoughts, and in your feelings. Play with different statements and thoughts, and see which ones feels right for you. You have free will, so choose what brings you peace, happiness, and love.

Lastly, I would like to share a simple yet powerful tool that Jim Self and Joan Walker shared, called *The Rose*. It helps us recognize the difference between our thoughts and emotions and those belonging to others. It serves as a point of delineation between your environment—your world—and everyone else's, so you can observe, choose, and respond, rather than react.

It's a space where you choose to experience yourself while not being affected by others. Imagine, if you will, creating a beautiful red rose. Imagine holding this rose and creating a circle around yourself. Everything on the inside of the rose is the energetic frequencies you are responsible for. Everything on the outside of the rose is Shakespearian theater for your enjoyment. This is a place where you do not have to be drawn into the dramas, the chaos, and the noise of what is going on in the world around you. This tool allows you to create life on your terms.

The last thing I would like to share is a quote attributed to Ralph Waldo Emerson:

What lies behind us and what lies before us are tiny matters compared to what lies within us.

About the Author

Katheen Bradley is an author, teacher, consciousness facilitator, Reiki master, Angel Therapy Practitioner®, interior designer, and founder of Kathy Bradley and the Angels. As a successful business owner for more than twenty-five years, Kathleen shares her insights, techniques, and guidance, inspiring her many clients to awaken to their true divine path and purpose. She provides practical tools to assist in consciously navigating the changing times into the New Paradigm.

The teachings offered are short and simple to use, specifically designed for those with busy lives.

The information she shares is a culmination of her studies, personal experiences, and channelings. Kathleen has presented many lectures in libraries and has offered special programs tailored to the spiritual communities that promote growth, healing, and conscious living.

Kathleen is married to her husband of thirty-seven years and happily lives on the East End of Long Island.

To receive a complimentary eBook, please email kathybradleyconsulting@yahoo.com or call 516-635-7248. To learn more, visit: kathybradleyandtheangels.com.

Katherine Brooke-MacKenzie

How has the Clickety-Clack shown up in your life?

I'd say my first major experience of the Clickety-Clack, which served to underpin a whole load of other Clickety-Clack exposure, was when my parents broke up. It was messy and upsetting for everyone, and I found myself left behind in the family home at the age of sixteen. I was desperately confused and traumatized by the way events unfolded. I didn't really understand the extent to which it affected me until my own life began to play out over time. In essence I was heartbroken, with issues around abandonment and big questions around whether or not I was really loveable. I found myself clinging to anyone who showed me kindness, which resulted in me being emotionally exploited and left me feeling even more desperate.

For many years, I made poor choices that impacted upon my health, physical and mental. I relied heavily on alcohol and got into relationships that were controlling, manipulative, and damaging for me. I generally felt unwell, depressed, and anxious a lot of the time until one day, I had a big wakeup call when I fell down the stairs in a drunken stupor. I heard a strong but gentle voice in my head tell me: *This is your life*, and I realized I had to make changes, or I was heading for a life in the gutter.

From that point onwards, I began to clean up my act and find myself the support I needed. I realized no one was coming to save me, and that my life, my health, and my choices were my responsibility. Turning that ship around was going to be a challenge, and I was scared by the enormity of the task, but it turned out to be an empowering and life-changing experience.

How did you navigate the Clickety-Clack?

I began to support myself with some complementary health therapies, initially using Traditional Acupuncture to reclaim my spirit, and then I chose a course of colon hydrotherapy treatments (colonic irrigation) to help me wipe the slate clean, as I felt dirty and ashamed of my earlier behavior.

I had to sort my shit out, and the colonic treatment helped clear out lots of physical and emotional crap I'd been carrying around for years. I purged my body of a lot of demons and cried my way through a huge emotional clearing, triggered by the treatments. I processed a lot of pain and a lot of anger. It was profound. I had no idea that my gut was hiding the secrets to my physical, emotional, and psychological wellbeing.

I also stopped running around to all my friends, asking their opinions about what I should do about everything in my life. I began to make my own choices and take responsibility for them, even if they went wrong occasionally. I learned about who I am and who I'm not, and I became clear about what I was prepared to accept for my life. I began slowly to love and respect myself, and my confidence began to grow as my personal boundaries strengthened.

What tools do you recommend for staying peaceful in a seemingly toxic world?

This may sound strange, but: *Learn how to parent yourself.* Most of us didn't have emotionally intelligent upbringings. Our parents did their best with whatever resources they had available to them, but it doesn't mean there weren't gaps. It is our responsibility as adults to have enough awareness to recognize the gaps when they show up in life and then fill them for ourselves.

When the shit hits the fan these days, I ask myself what I need in the situation. Sometimes it is simple self-care: a hot scented bath, a walk in the countryside, a nourishing, comfort-giving meal.

But other times require deeper self-reflection, and I imagine taking the part of me that is struggling with an issue out of my adult self. I put the struggling part into an image of a little-girl version of me. I sit her on my lap, I look into her beautiful innocent eyes belying the fear that hides behind them, and I love her. I hold her delicate, little body tight. I tell her she's safe and so important, and I thank her for bringing whatever the problem is into the light so that we can heal it together.

This exercise always moves me to tears. It's profoundly healing. It takes me out of the story—which was never real anyway—into something in the present and fixable. I've taken my little girl on all sorts of adventures, and she has done the same for me. Sometimes this process works the other way around because I realize I need the spontaneity and frivolity in my adult world that only a child can bring. Doing this has healed me in so many ways. It always works and helps me forgive myself when I self-attack or when I don't feel good enough. It also serves to stabilize me.

Try to cultivate an attitude of gratitude, appreciation, and wonder. During some real low points in my life, I depended upon these attitudes to keep my head above water.

Here is my nightly practice:

> I think of three things that went well for me that day, things for which I am grateful. I think of three people who were kind or who might have helped me or others in that day, and I imagine them standing in front of me. I picture my heart generating warmth, and I send it outward to their hearts with my message of appreciation for who they are as I give thanks for them.

> Then I think about something I don't know the answer to, something that is bigger than me. I ponder on the world, the human condition, psychology, space, God, angels, anything that I can't possibly grasp with my limited human mind, and I ask to be shown more miracles in my life. This keeps me excited and in the realms of possibility, and I highly recommend the practice.

Finally, I suggest you search your gut for the answers to whatever problem you're experiencing because this was pivotal to healing my life. The health of your gut controls a whole lot of hormones and neurotransmitters that influence your mood, mental health, and resilience. It also supports your immune system. It's so much easier to navigate any experience if you are healthy and well, so if you want to feel capable, comfortable, and confident to handle whatever Clickety-Clack comes your way, I highly recommend you start at the bottom and work up!

About the Author

Katherine Brooke-MacKenzie is an experienced colon hydrotherapist, PSYCH-K facilitator, EFT practitioner, and mBIT coach. She's studied Chinese medicine and has a BA (Hons) degree in Traditional Acupuncture. Katherine is also an author and international speaker on the subject of holistic gut health and runs a thriving gut health clinic in the southwest of England.

Katherine's personal experience and decades in the field of complementary health has enabled her to support thousands of people as they improve their quality of life through focusing on their gut health. She has spent countless hours researching; attending workshops, webinars, and therapies; and exploring what it means to be *healthy* within the realms of an individual's self-awareness.

Her empowering healing journey from broken to whole will inspire other health seekers to have the guts to live an authentic and naturally healthy life in line with their innate gut feelings and intuition.

If you're wondering how well your gut is working for you, please take part in a free gut health quiz available from her website thehealthygutclinic.co.uk, where you can also download her free eBook on colonics, *An Introduction to a Colon Hydrotherapy Treatment*. If you want to reach out directly, you can drop her an email at: hello@thehealthygutclinic.co.uk.

Cindy Costley

How has the Clickety-Clack shown up in your life?

The Clickety-Clack showed up in my life at the age of fifteen. It was then that I became allergic to everything, including most foods, chemicals, plant life, and all animals. For thirty-seven years, I went in and out of the Clickety-Clack with these massive allergic reactions and earned the title of *The Girl Allergic to the World*. I would be stable and doing well, and then suddenly, I was back in the Clickety-Clack, having an allergic reaction to something random; there was often no real rhyme or reason as to the exact cause of the allergic reactions.

These reactions came and went for thirty-seven years, each time calling for another Benadryl, cortisone shot, dose of prednisone, or antibiotic. Then five years ago, my body reached a point where it began shutting down; it could no longer handle the allergic reactions and the amount of disorder going on in my body. I knew I was dying. At that moment, I entered into a four-year Clickety-Clack process in which I surrendered to discovering the true reasons behind my body's disorder and choosing to heal my life.

As it turned out, the underlying causes were three incidences of trauma I had experienced as a child. The allergic reactions were my body's way of protecting me from getting hurt again, by keeping me away from everything and everyone. In my younger years, my body managed to bounce back relatively quickly, but by the age of forty-nine, the reactions had become constant.

When I went into that phase of the Clickety-Clack, I made a decision to no longer deal with these reactions—choosing to no longer live my life that way. I went into the Clickety-Clack to let go of suffering and to heal my life completely. In doing so, I went through this beautiful healing process over the next few years.

How did you navigate the Clickety-Clack?

Through the years prior to age forty-nine, when I decided to really let go and heal my life, I managed physical challenges by pushing through them. I ignored everything, any emotion or feeling behind it, and I just pushed through. I did not realize at the time that I was shoving emotions, feelings, and energy inward, so I moved past it with speed, commitment, and drive to live a better life.

But at age forty-nine, I realized that pushing through was not serving me. What I really needed to do was choose to go through each experience with ease, grace, peace, and love. I needed to learn to love and choose myself above everybody else. The first thing I did was choose to heal. I declared what I wanted. I knew from my heart and my soul what was possible for me.

Then, I sought out specialists. I added a spiritual teacher because I had seen many practitioners and physicians, both Eastern and Western, and I knew I needed to do it differently this time. I chose a spiritual counselor who helped me learn to listen to my body. I started to meditate. I listened to what I was being told and what my body needed from the inside versus the outside world.

I resonated with seeking answers from within and allowed myself to see the signs around me as to what my body truly needed. Then, I also learned to trust the Universe. When I sat in meditation and listened, I trusted. This was difficult for me because I had spent thirty-seven years not feeling safe in this world.

I entered a space of completely trusting the Universe. I focused on healing all aspects of my life: the physical, the emotional, the spiritual, and the energetic. Navigating that Clickety-Clack and moving through that space of healing had to do with all four aspects. Without any one of these, I was not in balance.

Then, I allowed patience with the process. I stayed focused on the day-to-day rather than looking too far into the future or too much in the past. I reached out for my support system when I needed. There were days that were unbearable, and I had my loved ones to support me through those times.

I also gave myself grace to have bad days. There were lots of days when I said: *You know what? Today is just one those bad days, so I am going to allow these feelings.*

Those are pretty much the basic steps I experienced as I have healed and gone through this last part of my Clickety-Clack.

What tools do you recommend for staying peaceful in a seemingly toxic world?

This is such a great question. The first step I take with my coaching clients is always **prioritizing *self* first**. I did not do that for many years. I prioritized my husband, my job, my kids, and my house. All that stuff! Prioritizing yourself is truly one of the most important steps that you can take for yourself.

The next step is **seeking answers from within**. It is easy to look outside and say: *Okay, this doctor needs to tell me what is right. This specialist needs to tell me what I need to do.* We often seek answers from a variety of professionals that other people tell us to consult, and the reality is: Nobody knows our body better than us. Nobody knows what you are going through and what your individual needs are better than you. The best answers are going to come from within you versus the outside world.

Then the third step is **staying grounded**. I do that through nature, where I can focus on staying out of my head and in my heart. The best way to do that is by being grounded to nature, to our world, to spirit. Make sure you are getting outdoors and taking those walks, putting yourself in nature and looking at the life force all around us because that life force is connected deeply to your soul.

If you are going through the Clickety-Clack and are not connecting to your soul, everything you do and every answer you discern is going to come from your head. You need answers to come from your soul and your heart.

Part of that process comes from **meditating daily**. That would be the next step in my answer, taking time to meditate daily. Then, practice grace with yourself. I did something well for myself these past few years. I granted myself grace for not being perfect and not doing it right. I did the best I could every day. Grant yourself this same grace. Take big, deep breaths and recognize you are doing all you can do in every moment.

Then the last piece when you are navigating the Clickety-Clack is **processing your emotions**. For thirty-seven years, I shoved all my emotions inward. That did not serve me in any way, shape, or form. I have learned over the last four years that getting in touch with those emotions—feeling your sadness, feeling your anger, feeling your hurt, feeling your pain—and allowing them to speak through you is the most healing thing you can do for yourself. It is vital that you let yourself feel the feelings your body wants to release.

About the Author

Cindy Costley is an integrative wellness coach, business owner, and entrepreneur. Her personal and professional journey has allowed her to empower her clients to take control of their lives and heal physically, emotionally, spiritually, and energetically. It has also provided her with a wealth of information on the various healing modalities available to assist those individuals who are stepping into bravery and saying yes to healing and being all they are meant to be in this world. Cindy's coaching style is informative and nurturing, and she is extremely passionate about working with clients who are committed to their process and willing to put in the difficult, yet rewarding, work to heal their lives.

Cindy's husband, three children, and three grandchildren all have her heart and allow her ample time to laugh and play through life!

Visit theunderlyinganswers.com to receive a free eBook and to learn more about her Healing Village Membership and Empowerment Course.

Dario Cucci

How has the Clickety-Clack shown up in your life?

One thing happened to me two years ago in London. I was invited to attend and speak at a conference, *The Men's Network*. The night before my speaking engagement, I stayed in an apartment. Around 9:00 p.m., I felt a feeling in my face for the second time in my life: I felt a crying feeling and part of my face grew numb.

I knew immediately what was happening. I thought: *Oh my God! I just had a Bell's palsy attack*, which meant part of my face, the left side, had been paralyzed. There was no movement on the paralyzed side, and my speech was not clear. I looked funny; I could not smile. It was not very attractive.

On the following day, I was supposed to be a keynote speaker at the event. I remember thinking to myself: *What am I going to do?* Most people are more afraid to speak in front of people than they are of death. The other thing people normally fear is looking funny or being judged. Even though I was facing both of these things, I ended up going to the event.

Now, everything that could go wrong went wrong on the day. There were delays. The sound was not working. There were only five guests, not the expected forty. Everything else was out of sync, and I was in front of people with part of my face looking funny, not able to speak as clearly. I decided: *I am not going to let this stop me. I am going to present and do the best thing I can do. I am here to serve the people.*

As soon as I thought those thoughts and focused on the guests that were there, my limitations did not matter anymore. At that moment, I had the right thought: *You know what? I am just going to deliver the content; this is why I coach people.* I chose to let them know I had Bell's palsy so they could tell me if they did not understand me so I could speak slower. As a result, the people enjoyed the training, and I actually gained a client from it.

When you are going through a challenging time and you stand up and believe in yourself, you can do anything.

How did you navigate the Clickety-Clack?

I navigate the Clickety-Clack through self-confidence. That confidence has been built as I have worked in the self-development industry for over fifteen years. First, I decided I was not going to let this disability stop me; I was going to serve people. Then, instead of criticizing myself for looking funny and not being able to speak as clearly as I normally do, I actually did the best I could with my knowledge and my resources, and I tapped into the knowledge I have gained. That gave me confidence.

Second, I went to a hospital to get medication to bring down the inflammation in my face. After I received the medication from the doctor, I knew I needed to do something to heal my body. I ended up visiting an acupuncture therapist, and I started the healing process on a deeper level to release the cause that brought this condition on and to heal my body at a cellular level.

I started a process of healing, and within two to six months, I was about 95 percent healed. I worked with myself, drank medicinal tea that was really awful to drink—like drinking black planet earth—and underwent hypnosis.

One of my friends who practices quantum healing reached out to me and offered me help. She helped my face using Rapid Transformation Therapy (RTT), which is a combination of timeline therapy, hypnosis, and quantum healing. Her work helped me let go of the disability of the Bell's palsy and to heal my face, so I could gain more movement. Now, I can smile again!

When something like this happens, do not listen only to Western medicine. Find a way to include alternative medicine and healing processes. Our bodies and our minds are complex, not black and white. We create everything in our lives, every disease. The truth is that, even if you do not like it, you created it. I created Bell's palsy for whatever reason.

When you acknowledge the truth about challenges in your body, you also heal the challenges because you are taking your power back, and that is the most important thing.

What tools do you recommend for staying peaceful in a seemingly toxic world?

One thing I share with people all the time is something I learned from Eckhart Tolle and from living my life in the present moment: *Do not think about the past. Do not compare yourself to the past or what you could have done in the past or even where you want to go in the future.* Instead, think about how you can do your best in the current situation, being content with who you are, where you are. Be thankful for who you are because there is only one you.

You are like a snowflake. When it snows, billions of snowflakes come down on Earth. Every snowflake looks similar; however, every snowflake is actually different. So is every person on this planet. Every person has a purpose in their life; that is why they were born.

When you finally know what your purpose is, then all the drama, all the distractions, all the things going on in life become insignificant because you know why you are here. When you know what your purpose is, you seek being at peace with yourself and who you are. You understand that all the stuff happening around you is feedback you can learn from. Then, it is a lot easier for you to stay at peace, coming from a loving place instead of from a place of fear, hate, and anger. Remember that people are in your life to guide you, to give you feedback, and to give you a way to learn more about yourself.

There are a lot of things happening right now in the world that lie outside our control. All you can do is focus on what you are grateful for in life. Center yourself. Be in the present, where you are right now, and focus on what you can do, your power. Use your life as a positive influence so it creates a ripple effect, bringing value to this world on a universal level. When you do that, you will not have time to get caught up in drama.

Relax and be true to yourself. Be in the present. Don't get caught up in the past or the future. Be in the present. Absolutely.

About the Author

After discovering that so many professionals, experts, and coaches struggle to get repeat business, Dario Cucci is now proud to dedicate his entire twenty-five years of expertise to help transform the mindset, communication skills, and business strategies of clients all over the world to support their growth.

His career in sales started within the self-development and events industries over twenty years ago in Australia when he worked with the Tony Robbins team as a sales executive, based on commission-only income. During his first year working with them, he generated over £1,000,000 of additional sales revenue for the company.

He applied his impressive strategies of earning multi-national companies annual revenue of seven figures in Australia for over ten years. After being continually bombarded with requests to explain the principles he used to create such results, Dario decided to make his techniques available by introducing and using his *High-End Sales CARE System*.

Dario went against the grain, moving away from the old-fashioned marketing campaigns and deciding to focus on helping his clients create new business from their most underrated assets, including their existing client bank where trust has already been created. Dario's unique approach and authentic coaching style has allowed him to create ripples across the world as he confidently delivers his message in such a way that business owners can implement his strategies with immediate effect.

He now provides training, coaching, and mentoring by holding live workshops, seminars, in-house group training, online group coaching, and one-to-one coaching.

Make an appointment with Dario Cucci and find out how he can help you improve your mindset to increase sales and grow your business, serving your customers better, at: dariocucci. net A chapter from his book, *Turn Your Customers Into Profit* is available for free. Download your copy of "Turning Objections Into Sales" also at: dariocucci.net.

Marie Diamond

How has the Clickety-Clack shown up in your life?

When you have a long career, the Clickety-Clack shows up several times, right? The time that stands out most in my memory was when I was living in Belgium. I felt like I had reached the highest level I could in that country. I had a big vision of reaching more than a million people, and I understood that if I stayed in Belgium, I would not be able to achieve that goal. I had to *jump*.

I needed to immigrate to America. When I arrived, I had six suitcases and a few thousand dollars with me. I was used to everything going forward easily, and I had been in the flow for like four, five years in my business.

Suddenly, I was at the point where I was in the Clickety-Clack. I wondered: *Wow! What is going on here?* I was not able to make the income I wanted. I was not able to connect with people. So that was, for me, the Clickety-Clack.

How did you navigate the Clickety-Clack?

I found myself in the land between two countries, a no man's land. I was thinking: *I cannot go back.* I could not move forward as I wanted, but going back was not an option. I felt I had already done all I could in Belgium, so that time was behind me.

Every day, I needed to reconnect with my goals, my vision. I started to meditate every morning on my vision:

I am here to enlighten more than five hundred million people.

Show me the way; show me how.

Bring me the people; bring me the solutions.

I was, of course, taking action every day, but I kept focusing on my gear for the next year, the legacy I wanted to leave. As I was meditating and focusing foward, things started showing up. People started showing up. A year later, I was on my way. I was asked to be in the movie *The Secret*. I started signing top clients. I started having a lot of students in my classes. It took me about a year to travel out of that no man's land.

When the Clickety-Clack showed up, I never gave in to despair; I focused forward on my vision.

What tools do you recommend for staying peaceful in a seemingly toxic world?

I find silence in myself through meditation, prayer, and walking in nature. Our toxic world is a world full of noise, opinions, and judgments. In order to move beyond that and find peace, the only way for me is to go inward—to go to that place of heart, that place of soul, that place of being—where there is no toxicity. In this inward place, there is only love, compassion, and nonjudgment. I journey to that place every day through the meditation given to me fifty years ago, *The Tubes of Light*.

In the last twenty-five years, I have shared my first tool, *The Tubes of Light*, with more than a million people. People practice this meditation every morning for five minutes and follow the four steps of this practice, which move them quickly out of toxicity.

In the *Tubes of Light*, people visualize:

1. White light, accepting their power to create desires

2. Royal blue light, accepting protection

3. Rose light, accepting love and support by people and the Universe

4. Violet light, accepting forgiveness for limitations and judgments

As a feng shui master, the second tool I use is creating a space that is harmonious, loving, and warm—not toxic. I teach people to create a peaceful environment, especially when the world around them feels toxic. Creating this space is what feng shui is truly about.

It is not always easy to raise the vibration in yourself. So, if you raise the vibration in your environment, you can raise your own vibration within that environment more easily, thus releasing toxicity. I recommend you start with decluttering, organizing your environment, and letting go of items you no longer need to hold. Clean up your space and add fresh flowers, beautiful candles, and crystals. Create an environment in which you feel at home, at peace. It is easier to be at peace in your home if it is a space of peace.

About the Author

Marie Diamond is one of the world's top transformational leaders, speakers, and bestselling authors. A renowned voice on Law of Attraction, she is a *Seer* in a modern context and the only European star featured in the worldwide phenomenon *The Secret*.

Marie merges her profound intuitive knowledge of energy and the Law of Attraction with her studies of quantum physics, meditation, feng shui, and dowsing to transform the success, relationships, and inspirations of individuals, organizations, and corporations. Her clients include billionaires, A-list celebrities, top-selling writers, motivational speakers, CEOs, Fortune 500 Companies, governmental organizations, and more than 300,000 students online.

Marie is a founding member of the Global Transformational Leadership Council. She is both founder and president of the Association of Transformational Leaders of Europe.

If you'd like to learn more about Marie's work and receive a free gift, please visit: mariediamond.com/energynumber/.

Brian Evans

How has the Clickety-Clack shown up in your life?

Like most of you, the Clickety-Clack has shown up in my life in large and small ways. Some ways are more inconvenient but easy to navigate, and some forms of the Clickety-Clack have just shown up as walls or mountains, seeming insurmountable. When talking about the Clickety-Clack in this book, I am talking about the big ones—the mountains and walls—because so many people face obstacles that seem insurmountable.

There are four qualities of the Clickety-Clack in these particular times:

1. The dark night of the soul, a night that feels like everything is absolutely going to fall apart.

2. A sense of helplessness, desperation, or hopelessness in which we really do not know what to do.

3. A surrender of all the tips, tricks, and devices that can get us through the small Clickety-Clacks but do not seem to work on the large ones.

4. A sincere asking for help because whatever we need to move through this big obstacle, this big Clickety-Clack

is on the other side of what we know and what we know how to do.

My experience goes back to 2016. I had left my corporate job at the end of 2015, and I was excited to coach full time. As I started down this career path, I was drawn by my vision. I felt strongly that I was here to serve, and this new career was going to provide for all my needs.

After about four months, I encountered money challenges that arose from transitioning from a W-2 job to an entrepreneurial endeavor. I found I was starting to abandon my vision. In fear, I was starting to run back into the things I had left a couple months earlier. Next came a sense of desperation, and I could not see my way out.

On August 25, 2016, I experienced my dark night of the soul. I had an argument with my wife about what I was going to do, and I truly did not have a sense of how to move forward with my next steps.

How did you navigate the Clickety-Clack?

In that one sleepless night, I navigated the Clickety-Clack by surrendering and asking for help. Asking was difficult because I had spent fifteen years helping others, and helping is in my nature. I find it far more difficult to ask for and receive help. But that night, I was driven to a point where I did not know what else to do. So from to 2:00 a.m. to 5:00 a.m., I posted on social media that I needed help. I sent texts to friends saying I needed help. I emailed everyone I knew. That was my moment of surrender, saying: *I need help.*

A coach I have known for fifteen years saw one of my posts in the middle of the night, reached out to me, and said: *Now I know why you have been on my mind so much. I would love to offer you a coaching call and see how I can help.* A couple of days later, I scheduled a call with her; that call changed my life. In sixty minutes, I completely reconnected to my vision and my purpose, the thing that drives me to serve others.

She said, "You can do it, and I will help you."

Simply hearing someone say: *You can do it, and I will help you* made all the difference in the world. Even though I was still tentative, I could lean into all the faith she had in me, borrowing her faith until I could feel my own. She encouraged me to take one small step, which I did. I sent an email to a small group of friends and said: *I am going into my coaching practice full time, and I want to offer help to anyone who is interested.*

Three friends wrote back within an hour saying: *Great! When can we set up a call?*

Having this coach in my life has been absolutely invaluable to helping me navigate the Clickety-Clack—the ups, the downs, the lessons—and the rides still keep coming. Working with someone helps me see what *is* and what *is not* and helps me navigate the Clickety-Clacks that emerge out of those moments when I decide to move forward in the way I am called.

What tools do you recommend for staying peaceful in a seemingly toxic world?

The tools I use and offer to my clients are designed to help us remain centered. There is so much going on, and without an anchor or root, it is easy to be swept up. There are several different tools I offer.

1. I encourage my clients to learn to let go because there is not a prize for suffering or for those who suffer most. Often, we keep creating suffering out of a misguided sense that we must keep going, but we do not. The wise know when to stop and move in a different direction. Simply put, if something is not working, stop doing it.

2. The second tool is asking for help. Most people are good at helping others, but they are not as good at asking for and receiving help. Before you move into crisis, write a list of all the people in your life who can help you in some way. You do not have to know *how* they might help. You know who they are; they are willing to help. If something happens, you will already have a resource list.

3. I tell clients to double down on what lifts them up. I have learned over the last couple of years that you should do the things you love *daily*, whether movement, creation, meditation, praying, journaling, or music—whatever that lifts you up is the way you can stay connected to the things that make you feel good, even if the world seems topsy-turvy.

4. I encourage clients to practice discernment. In a seemingly toxic world, especially one driven by social media and other opinion machines, be discerning with whom you share your dreams. The biblical passage about casting pearls before swine has never been more relevant than it is right now.

5. Find a guide. My coach literally changed my life. Luke Skywalker found Obi-Wan Kenobi and Yoda; Neo found Morpheus. Someone who can help us see things truly and differently is absolutely essential in our lives.

6. Finally, I share the snow globe effect. In the snow globe effect, all your stuff is settled, where it is supposed to be. Then, life comes along and shakes it up. Recognize that all the stuff swirling around you will come back and settle down again. You must wait and be patient, knowing the truth that it will settle down again.

I have become practiced at allowing Spirit to speak. I have guidance, bullet points, and thoughts, but I know there are some things I am going to say that I have not written. There are some things that I do not say that I have written, and I know there are a whole host of things that will be spoken through me that I have not even thought about. That is a beautiful gift for me, to step into that channeling space.

About the Author

Brian Evans is a certified executive, leadership, business, and transformational life coach. He established his private practice in 2004 and is headquartered in Los Angeles with clients worldwide.

Equally adept at coaching individuals in the spirit of matter and matters of Spirit, his varied clients include Fortune 500 companies, international hockey players, worldwide bestselling authors, stay-at-home moms and dads, C-suite executives, spiritual teachers, startup entrepreneurs, YouTube celebrities, sole proprietors, terrorism experts, Mary Kay reps, rocket scientists (astrophysicists), and NFL and NCAA athletes. His all-time favorite client is the crown prince of a Middle Eastern kingdom.

Brian is dedicated to the inspiration and empowerment of all people, everywhere. He coaches individuals and organizations to improve their lives and the lives of others, inspiring humanity to be, do, and live better.

To learn more and connect with Brian, visit:

BrianEvansCoach.com

Instagram, Facebook, Twitter: @BrianEvansCoach

Mention *Navigating the Clickety-Clack* in your message to schedule a complimentary vision/strategy breakthrough session designed to envision and create an inspired life you love!

Naomi Gillespie

How has the Clickety-Clack shown up in your life?

The Clickety-Clack has shown up many times in my life—when I was a little girl, and later, when I developed melanoma after I had my first child. I was born a happy human; I was born with joy. When I was six, some bad stuff happened, and I dealt with it.

However, the time I felt it in every part of my body was when I had a clinic and was working sixty hours a week. I was overweight, overwhelmed, and exhausted. I became a single mom and was alone, which was challenging. I lived in an outback town that was not my style. I am a rain-forest-beach girl, and this town was basically the desert.

During that time, I was blaming, looking externally. I hunted and blamed everyone around me for my situation and discomfort. I was blaming my job, blaming where I lived. I blamed everyone except myself. I lost connection with myself. In the process of losing myself, I lost connection with others. I lived in this massive bowl of stress and anxiety, and that bowl *became* me. I became reactive. I became highly strung. I became negative. The reason was I had lost connection with others and my spirit. My body, my mind, and my intuition had all left the building.

Sometimes, I was driving to work and wondered: *If I just turn off this road and run into that tree, will I die? Will anyone even care?* That is how bad it got, and that is how the Clickety-Clack showed up in my life. The emotions were so overwhelming they overtook my life; I did not care whether I was alive or dead. The Clickety-Clack was like the train coming, and it was going to hit me at the station.

When I was a little girl, I understood about universal energy, and I appreciated nature and everything around me. I was not born rich in money, but I was rich in love. As the oldest of five kids in the family, I understood from a young age to appreciate everything I had. It took me feeling exhausted, tired, overweight, and unloved to notice that the Clickety-Clack had shown up in my life.

I felt completely lost in this world, and I did not even know where *my place* was.

How did you navigate the Clickety-Clack?

I remember this distinctly; it was like an epiphany. I basically said: *Stop the bullshit, Naomi.* I woke up one morning and realized that life was passing me by, and I was not even living it. I was just in it. I thought back to myself as a child who was happy and strong and asked myself what I wanted from this life, how I wanted to live.

To everyone else, I was so successful. I was making lots of money; I was on the top of my game. I had a clinic that was booked out with a waiting list like all practitioners want. I thought I was happy, but all these things were on the outside. On the inside, I was dead. I had to make the decision to live, to wake up. I woke up and I realized I was not dead yet. I realized that other people were. People pass in their sleep and babies aren't always born, but I was not those people. *I was alive.*

I realized I was not being grateful, and I was not appreciating the Universe, anyone around me, or anything I was taught growing up. I was not honoring my life or myself. One day, I woke up and decided to be alive. My decision was everything. I chose to have feelings, and I searched down to the bare bones of my feelings of who I was. I chose to be happy and to practice gratitude.

As I came out of depression and overwhelm, I had to retrain myself. I had to teach myself to think positively again. I had to rethink everything that was creating stress for me. I had to drop my high expectations of myself and my imagined expectations of what people wanted from me. I needed to choose not to stress, not to worry, and choose instead to be positive.

I had to release my fear of the known and the unknown, and I had to learn to believe in myself again. I also needed to take time for myself. I had to choose myself because I had been choosing everybody else. I had behaved as a slave, a doormat, a servant because of my profession and my nature. I had always believed we are here to help other people, so I had become a helper.

It wore me out, and I forgot who I was. To move out of the Clickety-Clack, I had to choose me, choose to live, and choose to live with gratitude. I had to do it every morning as I woke up; I had to choose to have a remarkable day.

What tools do you recommend for staying peaceful in a seemingly toxic world?

When I had melanoma, I developed a methodology called *Stop, Drop, and Soul.* I thought I was going to die. This occurred before the overwhelm I just spoke about. I practiced this method until life got in the road, and I stopped doing it. Big mistake!

In Stop, Drop, and Soul, when you feel the energy of anxiety and stress in your body—even before thought comes into your mind—you make it stop. You drop everything in your mind and clear it, so you can *be* in that moment. It is about being present because that is where we truly live life, in each moment. Stop, Drop, and Soul—drop everything and get back down to how you are feeling, get back down to your soul, that intuition, that knowing that you have.

This is where you can realign your head, your heart, and your intuition and get back to your true self, so you can live that remarkable life in your mind. You can create the dream in your head, and then, you make the dream your reality. So to stay peaceful, I Stop, Drop, and Soul. It is like I put a bubble around myself and nothing else exists. I remain completely present, and I hunt for the imbalance. I can feel it because it is a feeling. I find the stress or another feeling, and then I replace it with some positivity. Then, I think about gratitude. That is all I do.

It is simple and you can do it! The secret is catching yourself in the first moments of stress, negativity, or that daily grind. If you want to feel bigger and better and greater, you have to focus on your own spirit. Find gratitude in every moment of the day by simply being present.

The other thing I do is spot the *disconnection.* If there is something in your life that is corrupting your spirit or creating grief or sadness in your heart, you must hunt for it. Your greatest place of joy is feeling love and connection and that you have a place in the world. The moment we feel we have a place in the world is when we experience calmness. We then have absolute peace within us, no matter what cyclone or chaos is going on around us.

When we have a connection to the ones we love and to ourselves, nothing else really matters. When we have true joy because we feel and give love, we have found the secret to life. If we can create connection by decluttering all the stress, hate, sadness, and unspoken words, we can actually have the conversations we are afraid to have. If we can step up, be brave, and create that connection and let go of grief and sorrow, we will once again live a remarkable life and feel joy.

I always say: *Be a purveyor of joy and the huntress of belly laughs!* I am a naturopath, so I know it is essential to eat well and exercise for our body. We must move to clear our head space.

The other thing I love to do with my people is declutter, declutter, declutter. So that you are decluttering your mind, remember to Stop, Drop, and Soul. You are decluttering your heart when you connect. You are decluttering your spirit when you are present in the moment. Declutter the space you live in. What you need to do is declutter your head, your heart, and your home.

Once you have all those elements aligned, life reaches out, so you have success and joy in other parts of your life. As simple as that sounds, it is true. We see it. There must be something to it, right?

These are my tools to help you get your funky monkey back and to start being the huntress of joy.

About the Author

Naomi Gillespie is a women's thrive expert, speaker, mum, and author. She runs women's empowerment and weight-loss programs using her unique *metaphase method*. She is passionate about life, striving toward greatness and pushing the boundaries of the norm. Her love for her work and the people in her care is unbeatable. Moments with Naomi are packed full of belly laughs and fun; they are never dull. Her scientific brain meshes with her empathic side to create the perfect combo for understanding what makes us tick and for helping others achieve results for the long term, so they can live their best life and be remarkable.

To book a chat: badassbeatthebulge.com/.

Contact Naomi on her Facebook page, *Abundance Health with Naomi—Live It*: facebook.com/NaomiLiveIt.

Deanna Hansen

How has the Clickety-Clack shown up in your life?

The Clickety-Clack is near and dear to my heart, actually. When I began this journey developing *Block Therapy* as a global enterprise, it was not with the intention of being an entrepreneur. I was gifted with an understanding of the body, so if I wanted to bring my innovation to the world, I had to wrap my head around creating a business in order to share this understanding with the masses. This has been a constantly challenging process within the Clickety-Clack because every step of the way has required something from me I had never done before, some challenge I had never encountered.

I view everything in the world, including the body, from a holistic process, which is what Block Therapy is about. It is a holistic practice. The body goes through what I call *a healing crisis*, and I see the Clickety-Clack has been part of the healing crisis for my business. For example, every time we start putting positive energy into the body, we create a disruption in the deeper adhesion and the deeper behaviors and patterns that need to be released. Within the healing crisis, it can appear that our health is being thrown backward. But really, it is a cleaning out of the body so that we can step into a new system and a new alignment that is stronger and healthier.

For the last twenty years of developing this business, I have been viewing it as similar to a healing crisis. Every time there is a need for a shift in the company—whether it is a big shift, such as bringing in a new team member or creating an entirely new system to support what we are doing—it is always fraught with a dis-ease and discomfort because every time we are doing anything, we are doing it for the first time. I understand that growth is happening during these times, and if we want to step into a new platform, on a new level, we have to push those limits of what is comfortable and encounter a whole new way of doing business.

I find it crucial to embrace the Clickety-Clack because when you do so, you are stepping into a greater freedom and opportunity in your business, so you can share your information with the masses in the most systematic and proficient way.

How did you navigate the Clickety-Clack?

I have absolute faith in my purpose and what I have been given to share. I feel I have been divinely guided for the last twenty years. This guidance has shown up so many times. In last-minute things that happened, I knew I was being supported. When challenging times hit, I could see the big picture and understand I was being universally supported and guided—being steered away from a path or moved toward a different set of experiences.

I hold this purpose and mission dear to my heart, and I truly believe God is directing this process. When I have encountered the Clickety-Clack, especially in extremes times with either my health or my financial situation, this guidance has been crucial. I trust that I have been given something valuable to share. That trust has been the best way for me to navigate hard times.

I also have had an incredibly wonderful support system of people around me through the years. I continue to attract the right people to help me on my path. Whenever I do not have answers to situations, I reach out to those smarter than me in their realms who can help or guide me. I feel a huge sense of safety within the community I have developed and with the associates I work with. They help me navigate those challenging times that I do not know anything about.

I am upfront with my community about the changes or delays that are coming. I let people know the challenges I am having and what I am doing about it, rather than sitting back and hiding behind the fear that I am not doing well or failing when delayed on a project timeline. I find being authentic and honest to those who are expecting results is the best path. People typically are forgiving. That to me is the biggest blessing, the community and the people.

So the three things basically are:

1. The **faith** in the mission
2. The **people** attracted to me through this process
3. The **community** I am developing

My community is here to receive the benefits of this system and to continue to give me guidance in a comfortable and safe-feeling way about what I need to move forward.

What tools do you recommend for staying peaceful in a seemingly toxic world?

Block Therapy is the practice I use to keep my own body and mind at peace. It is meditation, therapy, and exercise, all built into one practice. There are a couple different ways I approach my body with this work.

Initially, I began developing this practice with my hands. When I dive into my own body with my hands, I turn off the world and go deep into meditation. I connect strongly to my breath and listen to what my cells are saying. Block Therapy is a self-care version of that technique in which we rely on a handcrafted tool called the *Block Buddy.*

The results and the process are similar in this approach. You dive deep into the layers of your own body and connect to the cells deeper than you are consciously aware of, so you can hear what your cells are saying. You can actually put space back into your body to truly understand what is happening, what is causing the chaos, and what is the clearest path moving forward.

I am also an avid reader. I recently picked up *The Untethered Soul* again. Reading books that help bring me into the moment and see the bigger picture in life are crucial for my ability to stay grounded and present, especially when times are taking me into situations of chaos and frustration. If I pick up my book every morning and I read anywhere from a half an hour to an hour as I am getting ready for my day, it sets my intention to be strong in my understanding of what I need to do to bring the best day forward.

Once again, I value connecting to those who understand my path and have the ability to talk things through. I am a one-on-one person in relationships. I throw situations at people I trust and learn from listening to the opinions, experiences, and understandings granted in response. Those connections are important. The communication piece—getting stuff off your chest with those you trust—is an extremely helpful way to navigate stressful times.

I find reading is meditative for my brain, and the bodywork practices are meditative for my body. Communication, then, is a form of meditation in relationships. It all comes down to being present in the moment, allowing the mind to settle into a peaceful centered focus, so you can move forward in the healthiest way possible.

Hydrating, resting, and caring for yourself in ways required to keep you healthy in general are all necessary pieces to the puzzle.

About the Author

Deanna Hansen is a certified athletic therapist and founder of Fluid Isometrics and Block Therapy, a bodywork practice that is therapy, exercise, and meditation all in one. Deanna began her practice as an athletic therapist in 1995, always focusing on deep tissue work.

Deanna's work benefits people of all ages who experience any condition. Focusing on the fascia system, her work teaches people to melt through adhesions and scar tissue, ultimately awakening cells previously blocked from blood and oxygen. From those with debilitating issues to elite athletes, this work can be modified to address any situation.

Deanna has developed an online teacher-training program— Block Therapy University—so people around the world can teach in their communities and empower others to become their own health advocates. There are currently over 160 people globally who are either certified or in the certification process.

If you would like to learn more about Block Therapy, you can subscribe to her newsletter and receive a free copy of her book, *Fascia Decompression: The Missing Link in Self-Care* by visiting: blocktherapy.com/newsletter/.

Brigitte Keane

How has the Clickety-Clack shown up in your life?

There have been many Clickety-Clack moments in my life simply because I have been alive for a long time. Within those moments were many periods of waiting in which something new was happening, a new beginning. Like birth, new beginnings often need preparation time to be born. One of those Clickety-Clack times was my birth as the Laughter Liberator.

After many years as a laughter practitioner, I granted myself a wish I had for many years: to experience laughter activities in India where the original Laughter Movement started. From a humble beginning with five people in 1995, it has now spread all over the world. I signed up for a course with the Laughter Guru, Dr. Kataria. He lived in Bangalore, India, so off I went to Bangalore. The course lasted for two weeks, and I had planned to stay for three weeks. When I got back, I would arrive in New York, attend a seminar there, and proceed to my home.

On the day I was scheduled to leave India, I arrived early at the airport, even though my plane was not scheduled to leave until later that night. Upon arrival, I learned that travelers cannot just enter the airport in Bangalore. Passengers must wait outside the building and are only allowed into the airport three hours before departure—and then only if their names are on the daily flight list.

Fortunately, the weather was nice, and I spent all day around the airport. I even splurged and treated myself to a few hours stay in a luxury hotel. I learned they had a buffet with a special tropical fruit, mangosteen, a rare treat. I love mangosteen, the *queen of fruits*, and consequently, I filled up with this delicious fruit, ignoring many of the other delicacies.

Closer to departure time, I excitedly and anxiously waited in one of three lines. When it came to my turn, my name was not on the passenger list, so, of course, I could not get into the airport nor be on my flight back to the U.S. Imagine, me, a single woman, alone at night at an airport, finding out I will miss my flight. I was worried about my safety. I was in a strange country and fear kept creeping up. What was I to do?

Later, I found out what had happened. Instead of looking at the time when the plane was to leave, I had looked at the time for the plane to arrive. I took responsibility for that. The departing flight had two empty seats left; however, the cost was way out of my budget. There was no choice; I could not get on the plane.

How did you navigate the Clickety-Clack?

What was I going to do? I did not know anybody around here, except Dr. Kataria, who was the leader at the laughter seminar. I decided: *Okay, let me call him.*

I will never forget. When I called him and described my situation, he started laughing and laughing and laughing. I, of course, did not feel like laughing at all. Finally, he stopped laughing and listened to what I was saying. His response was simply, "Well, that just means you have to stay in India longer."

He made arrangements for me to stay for a few days at his office.

Instead of staying in India for three weeks as I intended, I ended up staying for six months! I had absolutely no plans for what I was going to do. I planned to go home and stop for a seminar in New York. I had absolutely no inclination to stay in India, but I needed to confront my new reality. I had to be flexible. I explored different opportunities. My host, Doctor Kataria, kindly gave me names of places he thought I would enjoy visiting.

I also called a friend in the United States who had many contacts in India, as she was an avid traveler. I informed her I was *stuck* in India and asked if she knew places or people for me to contact. To my surprise, she was coming to India herself. We got to meet and travel together.

One thing led to another. I got to experience many exotic places and even ended up *interning* at an acupressure clinic in Delhi where I became part of their healing team. There were many Clickety-Clack periods in between before I returned to the U.S. on the last day of my visa.

Sometimes things happen in our lives that do not go the way we want them to go, and often they surprise us. We do not have enough imagination to envision what our Clickety-Clack moments bring us. When I was pastoring a church, one of my church members told me about her mother who changed because she joined the Laughter Movement. She went from being highly critical and whiny to a much happier person.

At this point, I had not heard about the Laughter Movement but was, of course, aware of laughter. I did some research. When this church member asked whether we could incorporate laughter exercises into our Sunday services, she volunteered to be the leader. We agreed to have a laughter circle every Sunday after service. This was a very unorthodox idea in those days, and we were probably one of the first churches to offer regular laughter exercises.

I was surprised that people who would not participate in the service would participate in the laughter activities. We were teaching laughter without relying on jokes, humor, and comedy. While I have nothing against these activities, I believe that laughing for no reason causes laughter to become therapeutic. This belief continues to be validated in my experience.

What tools do you recommend for staying peaceful in a seemingly toxic world?

The tool I recommend to you is laughter. Laughter is your superpower. Laughter reconnects you to yourself. Laughter brings joy into your life. I am talking about laughing for no reason. We are not laughing at people, but with people. If you can learn to laugh at yourself, then you can deal with any situation.

Laughter has many health benefits for us as emotional, spiritual, and social beings. Do you know that every time you laugh you will improve your immune system?

Another tool I recommend is the Laughter Lifestyle. What is the Laughter Lifestyle? Simply said, it is a lifestyle spiced with laughter.

Here is an acrostic to remember the Laughter Lifestyle:

L — Live authentically and lighten up.

A — Access laughter as your superpower.

U — Understand and appreciate where you are in life.

G — Give yourself permission to play; giggle your way to joy.

H — Hope for the future; something better is on its way.

T — Take time to embrace the journey.

E — Empower and reinvent yourself.

R — Reignite your wisdom.

Laughter will reconnect you with yourself. When you laugh, a lot of things happen to your body physically, spiritually, emotionally, and socially. Laughter leads to transformation—I guarantee it.

Another tool I recommend is to respond rather than react. Stand back and respond to the situation. In my situation, I could have become really flabbergasted that I missed this flight. Instead, I had gratitude for this situation and whatever else happened so I knew that I would be okay.

I called my friend, and he laughed at first. I really did not feel like laughing. Once I arrived at his home, I stepped back and was able to plan my next steps. Everything works out. Always. Remember that you are never alone because a lot of good people are around you.

About the Author

Brigitte Keane, the Laughter Liberator™, will make your heart smile.

She is an internationally renowned healer, speaker, educator, and consultant, as well as the creative visionary behind Laughter Liberator: Pioneering the Laughter Lifestyle.

With more than twenty years' experience traveling the world as a laughter professional, Brigitte is passionate about sharing the healing power of laughter. Inspired by the life-changing experiences in her own life, Brigitte invites others who are imprisoned by the grind of daily life to play and experience the liberation of the Laughter Lifestyle™.

Brigitte's mission is to improve self-esteem, self-confidence, happiness, and the mental, spiritual, and physical health of people around the world. She believes that by supporting each other and laughing together, the world can become a win-win place filled with resilient people who can live a fun and liberated life through any situation.

To experience a video of Brigitte and her joyful energy, visit: speakerspathway.com/brigitte-keane/

Lidia Kuleshnyk

How has the Clickety-Clack shown up in your life?

I have had many experiences of the Clickety-Clack in my life, but the most life-changing was when I was ten years old. I was chronically ill, born with deformed internal organs. I experienced a lot of pain and suffering in my youth. I was in and out of hospital with doctors and procedures, but I did not have a lot of family support.

My family loved and cared for me, but they did not know how to navigate through that world. The age of ten was a turning point for me in becoming more self-empowered. That was my first Clickety-Clack experience. I was in a lot of chronic pain; I had severe digestive conditions. I would be well, then not well, as I went through the regular medical system.

Doctors tried to help me, but they were not able to. The turning point came when doctors told me it was in my head—I was imagining it and I should just go home and die. I did not take their words to heart. I believed there was a way for me to get out of the situation, heal, and get better. That whole experience at the age of ten set me on a course toward a life of healing and self-empowerment.

How did you navigate the Clickety-Clack?

I heard the expression, *If it is to be, it is up to me,* and I realized I had to be self-reliant and self-responsible, instead of entering into self-blame. I was conscious of blaming thoughts. I learned to rely on my inner self and those inner resources that we all have.

We are born with intuition, instinct, fortitude, natural skills, and gifts. I committed to knowing I would find a way out of my seemingly hopeless, powerless situation. Children are naturally dependent on everybody, but I did not want to be sick and dependent the rest of my life. My goal was to become a healthy independent person and be healthy like everybody else.

We lived on a farm in the country in the mid 1970s. We had a TV with three channels. In the small school library, I found three books: *The Power of Positive Thinking* by Norman Vincent Peale, *Lord of the Rings,* and *Little House on the Prairie.* Those books became my bibles for self-empowerment, directing me, and I pulled quotes and affirmations from them. I put these words everywhere in the house, including my light switch, to keep my mind focused so that I could elevate myself out of my experience.

When I was in a lot of physical pain, I would say, "My body is in pain, but I am not." Nobody taught me that. The experience of going through that pain activated that knowing within me. Ultimately, I learned it was a Daoist, nonattachment approach, but I did not know what Daoism was at the time. I thought: *short-term pain, long-term gain.*

I had no doubt I would achieve my goal. I focused my mind, and I spent time in nature. I had a fort in our ravine where I connected with the birds, the trees, horses, and dreams. Animal spirits came to me in dreams and talked to me. They came to me as pillars of white light, and to this day, horses come to me as pillars of white light and talk to me in dreams.

Through my spiritual connection and aligned action, I allowed a path to come forth. I started changing my diet because my health conditions manifested with digestive and endocrine disorders. I never felt emotional or mental strain; it was always stress at the physical level. I used my mind to bring forth and carry my physical body, using my mental strength and my emotional balance.

I never took circumstances personally—not my external circumstances of doctors nor my family who did not know how to help me. I just thought: *I have to figure it out myself.*

In macrobiotics, our teacher Michio Kushi said, "Sometimes, you need to have the mind of Sherlock Holmes to get through [the Clickety-Clack] and find your own solution." For every problem, there is a solution. Sometimes you must work a little harder and align yourself with your essence and your spirit in order to find the right solution.

My commitment to knowing I would find a way out and have a totally new life was my solution. I said to myself at the age of ten: *I did not come on the planet to be half-alive. I did not come on the planet to be struggling with basic physical functioning.* It was not acceptable to me. I went forward and kept trying.

What tools do you recommend for staying peaceful in a seemingly toxic world?

What I did at the age of ten, I carried on throughout the rest of my life. I experienced difficult times and challenges, having the rug pulled out from under me. When it happened again and again, I felt self-empowered because I had already had a similar experience, so I understood the process.

I journal and self-reflect. I also meditate, seeking to be honest about the circumstances I am in. If I can take time to be clear and honest about the circumstances I am in, then I can create a sacred space for personal manifestation to happen and can find available, unique solutions. I connect to my intuition by journaling and self-reflecting, knowing that for every problem there is a solution. *If it is going to be, it is up to me.*

I practice self-responsibility, but not self-blame. Affirmations and quotes keep my mind focused, and I put them everywhere I can when going through a Clickety-Clack.

The macrobiotic healing has been phenomenal. I have had dreams telling me about macrobiotics. I first heard about macrobiotic healing practices when I was ten, during that crisis in my life. In macrobiotics, food is nutrition and energy, so it helps you to be centered, connected, and conscious, to find peace. The whole basis of macrobiotic philosophy is that inner peace creates outer peace and world peace.

I recommend:

- Reiki energy healing
- Yoga
- Being in nature with animals, horses, stones, and trees
- Not personalizing external stressors

You are not what happens to you; you are what you make out of it. An external stressor is a catalyst for you to activate your inner power and connection with infinite energy.

There are something like one hundred billion stars in our Milky Way galaxy and one hundred billion galaxies in our universe. I can access all that energy when I am peaceful, centered, connected, and conscious. One of my affirmations that has gotten me through the Clickety-Clack: *I create my highest quality experience in any circumstance.*

There is no self-blame. Things happen, and we have self-responsibility in our response. Do not take on other people's actions as your own. *Discern and deflect external stressors.* Discern and then deflect, so you do not absorb the energy coming in, and you can stay strong, empowered, and then peaceful.

About the Author

Lidia Kuleshnyk, BSc, MES, is a chronic health specialist and creator of the Chronic Health Breakthrough Program™, a healing program to help overworked, stressed-out, high-achieving men and women resolve their chronic health conditions and achieve their health and wealth potential.

In private practice for twenty-three years as a health and energy coach, Lidia helps people who are frustrated and depleted become grounded and energized, so they can *Reclaim* their health, *Regain* their energy, and *Refine* their power. Lidia supports clients in their healing journeys through serious health conditions, including anxiety, arthritis, auto-immune conditions, cancer, concussions/brain injuries, COPD, digestive conditions, grief, heart and stroke conditions, and injuries. Lidia's passion for healing activates the energetic potential of her clients, so they feel empowered to heal and achieve their highest quality life.

Lidia is the creator of The Apona Healing Method™, the Turn Stress Into Success: 3 Steps to Regain Your Energy and

Reclaim Your Power™ program and The Capacity Principle™ of conscious leadership and success.

Lidia is most passionate about empowering conscious leaders to feel secure and confident in their knowing that they can turn any crisis or situation into success and activate their human potential to turn lead into gold.

To book a consultation with Lidia, visit: aponahealingmethod. com/copy-of-home or email her directly at: Lidia@ AponaHealingArts.com.

Gwen Lepard

How has the Clickety-Clack shown up in your life?

I had the most amazing experience of being on three telesummits, back-to-back. I thought this was a good thing. I said to myself: *I can share my experiences and my magic to help so many empaths.*

Because I was new to telesummits, I didn't know I needed time to promote each one of them individually. Some of these events have contracts stating presenters cannot be on another telesummit within two weeks. Most content, promotions, and offers should need approximately a month and a half in order for new people to follow through—instead of stacking events one on top of another.

It was not only the content and marketing that were draining because they were too close together, it was also the energy required to deliver on these telesummits. In one, there were some challenges with the platform, and it was moved to another date, which worked and was helpful. For the first one I actually ended up doing, I only needed to create a workshop. I created that, and I thought it was going to be easy. They said: *We only need you to create a workshop.*

However, I had to create all the facets needed in a telesummit. There was a lot going on. Because I was on three different telesummits, I had to create three different offers because they needed to be different yet still speak to the empaths I support. I was feeling super, super overwhelmed.

I thought: *Why did I say yes to this one?* I knew it was going to be tight, and they knew it was going to be tight. My email contacts asked: *How can you be constantly on these telesummits? Why should we go to this one? Why should we go to that one?* I caused a lot of confusion and Clickety-Clack in the inboxes of my empaths as well because I was not giving myself space to allow each telesummit to be a jewel by spacing them out a few months or doing only one per quarter.

When I spread out these events, I can bring the best of me and the best offering I have instead of hitting participants over the head with all these different telesummits. If I say: *I am here and I am here and I am here*, I am contradicting my own lessons about how to be unshackled, live freely, and evolve beyond energy bullying and narcissistic abuse.

I wanted the visibility so much, and it came to me so fast because I was experiencing success. So more and more people were saying: *We want you.* It was too much, too fast to do on my own.

How did you navigate the Clickety-Clack?

The first thing I did to navigate this *too much, too fast* was reschedule one of the three telesummits. But, I still did them all. I trusted myself to be creative and still bring exactly what was needed to those listening and felt *yes* in their hearts, to be drawn to work with me. I trusted I would show up in my full power for each and every telesummit.

I brought in a virtual assistant to help create the content, creating each event's separately so that I was not thinking: *Everything is bleeding over. Which telesummit am I on?* I needed to be clear: This is for telesummit one, this is for telesummit two, this is for telesummit three. As we created the content, she separated it in front of me so I could see exactly what I was offering for each of them and how it all wove together.

It also helped me create three separate products I could offer in the future. I was creating content to support empaths from the telesummit and for anyone who found it later as well. The process opened up my abilities to be creative, seek support, and to show up for my commitments in a powerful way. It expanded me as a speaker, as a mentor, and as a transformation facilitator in a way I had not imagined.

I was put in a pressure cooker of so many people saying: *Come, come. We want to share your message with our tribe.* In the future, I will say no more often and make sure events fit in my marketing schedule first so that for every summit I go on, I am able to bring along my people, and they can be excited, saying: *We have not seen you on anything in months! We really want to be there.*

I want those who follow me on different platforms to be able to think: *We haven't seen Gwen for a while. I wonder what she is up to now?* instead of: *Oh, Gwen again. Did I not just hear her in that other telesummit?* I choose to allow myself the space to share my message in a powerful way rather than thinking: *I have to do it now. Strike while the iron is hot.*

I learned the power of receiving help from somebody who is really organized.

What tools do you recommend for staying peaceful in a seemingly toxic world?

One of my favorites tools is **movement**. You can change your emotional state by changing your body. If you sit a lot, use the practice of setting a timer so, at least every thirty minutes, you get up and stretch. I like to put on music and dance. If you're feeling overwhelmed, notice how your body is doing: Are you all crunched over and having trouble breathing?

Sit up straight—or stand—bring your arms back, and breathe in a great big breath. Smile, even if you don't feel like it. All of a sudden, you will feel different. There is so much power in how we are in our bodies and having that awareness is really important.

The second tool I love is **feeling** your feelings. Put your hand on your heart and breathe. Notice any emotion you feel in that space between your hand on your heart.

Are you in the Clickety-Clack space?

I did this last night, overwhelmed with so many things. I thought: *I am in the Clickety-Clack. What can I do?* I put my hand on my heart, started breathing, and asked myself what I felt. I felt a sadness. I was able to say, "I feel sadness." Then, the feeling dissolved. Feelings want to be felt, and then they will leave. Instead of saying, "I *am* sad," as that creates more feeling of sadness. Instead, say, "I feel sadness." Then the sadness softens.

Next, I asked if I felt anything else. I felt angry. What else did I feel? I felt frustrated. Ah, frustration. I did a little scream. What else did I feel? I felt trust, and I was able to go back to work. That exercise did not even take a minute of time, maybe thirty seconds—breathing with my hand on my heart, feeling my feelings.

If there is a big, hairy thing in front of you, you may have so much fear, so much anxiety, that you may not know what to do. **Writing** it out is amazing.

Start with:

> *Dear Higher Power* (or whatever you call it),
>
> *I resent* (so and so, or such and such), *because I have fear that I* (whatever you fear).

Write for as long you can. Sometimes, I write for fifteen minutes; then when I am done, I complete it with:

> *Thank you, Higher Power* (your name or your higher power, or your source, your universe). *Thank you for removing these fears for me and anyone they affect* (you can add names). *I only ask for the knowledge of your will and the courage to carry it out. Thank you. Amen.*

Then, I ask my Guides to listen, and I read it out loud. Then I tear it up and put it in the garbage to get it out of the house, out of my office. This tool allows all those fears to leave; they are all dealt with. Then, I can move forward in a powerful way.

About the Author

Gwen Lepard is a radiant relationship luminary who empowers empaths to evolve out of energy bullying or narcissistic abuse. She supports empaths all over the globe as a Baggage Begone™ transformation facilitator, creator of the Lepard Method™ certification program and a mentor. She helps others release relationship residue, realize self-love, and regain personal power so they can have the love, peace, and freedom they desire. What she's most passionate about is helping create radiant relationships that stand the test of time.

She's an international speaker, award-winning broadcaster, and co-author of bestsellers, *Evolutionary Healer* and *The Gratitude Book Project*. She has appeared on numerous telesummits, including the Life Transformation Summit, You Wealth Revolution, and the Light Warrior Radio Show.

Visit gwenlepard.com/clickety-clack for a meditation to clear the Clickety-Clack and raise your vibration.

Adam Markel

How has the Clickety-Clack shown up in your life?

For me, the first sign of the Clickety-Clack was when I was maybe five or six years old. My parents moved, and I started living in a new neighborhood and was bullied pretty quickly. It was the first time I was hanging out or outside as a little kid, and there was another group of kids, a little older, and they bullied me. That was probably the first sign that life might not be quite what I first thought.

I would not have any expectation of what life was about at the age at all; I mostly trusted. That was the first time my trust in life, my trust in the universe—and now, I would have no qualms about saying my trust in God—was shaken. There was just no way to understand human beings being cruel one another. There is no way to explain to a five-year-old child why they would be attacked, ostracized, rejected, or abandoned.

At that time, I could not understand anything except to believe for the first time the world was not safe. Perhaps I also believed there was something about me that was wrong. Of course at five, six years old, there is not a lot of operational cognitive activity going on. We do not begin to develop this phase of cognition until around age eight. So I was making meaning out of it at an early age in which my thinking included my sense of self, of safety, of my worth in the world, and even what love meant at that time.

How did you navigate the Clickety-Clack?

With respect to this first incident of the Clickety-Clack in my life, I did not navigate it well. How could anybody navigate that well? However, I started to change my behaviors. I was fearful, seeing the world as a place where I needed to be afraid on some level.

I developed issues with trust, trusting in others, trusting in the Universe, or even trusting in myself, for that matter. Distrust became real for me as a result of not knowing whether or not I would be bullied if I went outside. As it turned out, the experience toughened me, and the toughening process help me develop resilience.

I do not know that I would choose to have developed resilience as a result of something like bullying, and I certainly would not want that to be the proving or developing ground for my kids or anybody else as they navigate growing into this world. But for me, it definitely developed my sense of alertness, my sense of being *on guard*. Ultimately, I needed to confront the demons, confront my fears of my surroundings, of other people, and of trusting myself and whether I was able to take care of myself.

As a child and into early adulthood, I developed the capacity to navigate these challenging situations, and then ultimately, I became an attorney and a business owner. Bullies appeared in many places. Those early experiences were mirrored later on in my practice of law as others took the role of the bully in my firm and in adversarial cases. I have seen the bully show up in politics, on the other side of business transactions, and as an attorney in adversarial litigation situations.

I discovered as a child that the *bully* is a *thing*, not a person with an assigned pronoun. When you stand up to that thing, the bully, you find out a great deal about yourself, of course, and you find out a great deal about the thing itself. A bully is in many ways an illusion; in many ways it is a smoke screen. It is a representation of fear.

My own experience has taught me quite well that when you face fear, it fades, dissipates, and shows itself to be made of nothing. It is, in many ways, an illusion. You can call that illusion *evil* or anything you want, but it is not, in fact, real. The stories we all make up about what scares us and where we do not feel safe and secure are really just that—illusion. These stories are part of the fear-based aspects of our mind.

While not a pleasant situation at all, learning to deal with the bullies early in my life not only developed resilience in me, but it has helped me help a lot of other people to develop that resilience, to develop the ability to face down their fears.

What tools do you recommend for staying peaceful in a seemingly toxic world?

Peace is something we are born with, and then, as life happens around us and within us, our peace is shaken; our peace is broken in many ways. Our trust in this natural state of peace is challenged in many ways through events that happen to us, people around us, and in situations we see in every context, every day—especially now.

Remaining peaceful is something we have to work at; we have to create peace for ourselves. It is not a default state of being for many, many people. If we can get back to the original factory settings for our soul, we can be peaceful, but in the world we live in, there are so many things that take us out of our peace. So, we have to create practices; we have to be vigilant and alert to the opportunities to be peaceful even in the midst of raging seas or storms of every kind.

The most important element I bring to each day is a calm. That is my intention: to bring calm to my experience of being for the day. I intend it and I start my day with a practice I call *the code of conduct* in which I basically sit for a few minutes thinking and saying out loud how I want to experience myself being today. One of the experiences I am grateful for in advance of its manifestation is: *I will experience myself as a peaceful being today.* In fact, this morning when I woke up, I said: *I am peaceful. I am the embodiment of peace today.*

We start with desire and intend those desires to be our experience of being and living. My life experience tells me we attract what we ask for, and that is ultimately what shows up in our experience each day. So many people do not ask specifically for states or experiences of being they are capable of in their life day by day.

The tools I recommend to anyone would be that you create—by intention, by design, by practice—the states of being you wish to live in. Start each day that way. As my grandmother would say: *Start on the right foot.* This *right foot* might for you be prayer or meditation or the practice I described as the code of conduct. Then in the evening, check in before bed to see whether that morning's intention was your experience for the day.

When we get to the end of this life experience, I believe we will feel only one thing as we are making that transition. That one thing is the way our life felt, day by day. We will feel the resonance of how we experienced living and being every day that preceded that final day. We will not take any possessions with us; we are not going to take anything other than our *felt experience of being.*

We might as well be working on that, being deliberate and intentional about creating experiences of being while we have the ability and the freedom to do so.

About the Author

Adam Markel is an international speaker, bestselling author, and executive business mentor who works with organizations and individuals to create high performance strategies and resilient work cultures that lead teams forward in times of change.

After building a multi-million-dollar law firm, Adam reinvented his own career path to become CEO of one of the largest business and personal growth training companies in the world. Adam credits much of his success to the principles he learned as a Jones Beach lifeguard in New York. He's found that the kind of leadership, resilience, and high performance required to handle 100,000 people on a crowded summer beach—with over 100 rescues each day—equally applies to any business that wants to build a competitive advantage to win.

Adam is currently the Chief Executive Officer of More Love Media, Inc., a company that works with individuals and organizations to build work cultures of greater unity, resilience, and connection. Adam's keynotes, corporate workshops, and business mentoring combine his "Lessons from the Lifeguard

Stand" with practical business strategies, personal development insights, and a unique delivery style to create a high-energy and impactful learning environment.

Adam's latest book is the bestselling *PIVOT: The Art and Science of Reinventing Your Career and Life.* Adam also hosts *The Conscious PIVOT Podcast,* where he shares his insights on pivoting in today's fast-paced marketplace.

For more information, visit AdamMarkel.com.

Jason Daveon Mitchell

How has the Clickety-Clack shown up in your life?

In the human experience, I have inevitably found that the Clickety-Clack is everywhere. I see moments in my childhood when I was trying to dial my way through the Clickety-Clack. As I examine my teenage years, I can see where I might have been trying to search my way through the Clickety-Clack. So, I find the Clickety-Clack is a natural aspect of the journey.

We are constantly moving through the known and the unknown. We are moving into a world flowing with constant information beyond the messages nature is sending us, beyond the nature of our own conscious communication with the self. The internet, our friends and family, social media, and traditional media are constantly sending us messages.

One of my biggest intersections of Clickety-Clack in recent years has been moving through my ministerial studies in the International Spiritual Center. Navigating the space between answering a calling to minister, the spiritual teachings of new thought, ageless wisdom, and of enjoying the joys and pleasures of life, I have found a constant expression of information at every turn. On that journey, the biggest challenge was honing the clarity of what I would write for my ministerial thesis.

The crushing energy of information, responsibilities, duties, callings, and desires all found me. I found myself in a space where I was not sure which decision I was supposed to make because they all sounded good or meaningful and had value. But I was aware of them all simultaneously at times, and then, I needed to pause.

How did you navigate the Clickety-Clack?

I found myself looking *outside* myself at all the books and information. I was quickly distracted by the major events happening over the course of the year, 2020. I was going every which way but in. I was taking me away from myself.

I was crushed by all the books I was flipping through and the web pages and browsers and apps I was searching. I was actively engaged in discovering my ministerial thesis and how I would be serving ministry once I was actively doing the things that were valuable and important for me to do. It was essential for me to be still, to become present.

The first thing I had to do was listen to myself and be still. The second thing was not just to meditate, but to become aware of everything I was doing and not doing. The next step was to go into meditation. Once I became present, I sat in my meditation practice and shifted into the practice of visioning—not just visualizing or picturing—but allowing all the information I had received to create a clarity that allowed me to see the path forward. I became present, available to the stillness, and then allowed the information I was gathering in those moments to create spaciousness.

What tools do you recommend for staying peaceful in a seemingly toxic world?

I recommend all available tools because I believe the uniqueness of human beings shows us that there is no singular way. The first tool I recommend is spending time in the silence. That time might look like formal meditation by sitting cross-legged; sometimes it looks like simply sitting down somewhere, eyes open or closed, not a formal meditation. Sometimes it looks like tuning out the entire world and putting on music that activates and inspires, raising energy.

Sometimes, the silence looks like a brain dump. Often, we have so much going on in our head that we cannot find our way through. Our thoughts are often like pulling out a piece of paper or opening up a computer document and typing nonstop, ignoring punctuation and spelling and paragraphs, simply expressing what is flowing.

I recommend more than anything that you reflect on your own life. See if there is a space within you where you have found peace. Now, it is perfectly possible that you will not be able to find one. We are all different, and some of us have lived in constant states of anxiety, stress, and challenge. However, if it is possible for you to reflect on a moment on your journey when you found peace, see if you can navigate your way to an awareness of what was going on in your life before that.

Were you dealing with a challenging relationship that looked like the Clickety-Clack?

Were you dealing with a change in job, a change in the economy, or even the way your change might have been changing?

If you can navigate to the space before, the time before time, you may find a key to your own peace. You may find where you disconnected. You may find how you reconnected. You may find that you rediscovered a passion. You may realize there was a time when you discovered some things were not nearly as important as others.

But one thing I know for sure—there is an aspect within you that is peace. Along this journey, you may have been living moments, windows, or episodes of pure peace that you have not noticed. I invite you to discover them.

About the Author

A native of Los Angeles, California, Jason Daveon Mitchell was nourished culturally and spiritually in the bosom of the Los Angeles basin. Born into a family of ministers, his spiritual journey represents a perpetual exploration of the Infinite. After more than a decade working as a teacher and then serving the skid row community of downtown Los Angeles, he answered the calling to life as an Agape Licensed Spiritual Practitioner, graduating in 2012.

For more than eight years, Jason has facilitated *Our Daily Prayer Call* (ODPC), a morning community call to prayer. On an average day, Jason and nearly one hundred people come together online and through teleconference to begin the day in prayer. As more people began to participate in ODPC, it became clear that there was a call from the community and the world for a greater relationship with Spirit by communing through community prayer.

A recent graduate from the Michael B. Beckwith School of Ministry, Jason continues to see clients, facilitate workshops, and speak around the country. He reminds people the world is a much better place when we come together, take our loving practices out into the world, and live them through our daily lives.

To be added to the ODPC email list, send an email to consciouslens@gmail.com. To attend *Our Daily Prayer Call*, visit: facebook.com/groups/OurDailyPrayerCall.

Cassie Schwind

How has the Clickety-Clack shown up in your life?

The Clickety-Clack has shown up in my life a lot of times, mainly in the crossroads where I had the chance to become something different or more of myself. One particular Clickety-Clack moment in my life was a living metaphor. I was driving home from university, preparing to change lanes. I caught my eyes in the rear vision mirror, and I had a moment of absolute truth. I realized I was unhappy; I saw it in the depths of my eyes.

I had to pull off and allow myself to sit with that moment because for all intents and purposes, I had this amazing life, a good life. I was studying. I had a business. I had a relationship. We had a great house. My life from the outside was fantastic, and up until that moment, I thought it was fantastic as well.

When I started to change lanes on this highway, I changed lanes in my own life. The Clickety-Clack ground me to a halt because I had to sit with the big truth of myself and be honest about who I was and the life I was living. Although I had a good life, I was not living my great life. I was not living the calling I had felt since I was a little girl. I admitted what I wanted to contribute. I sat in that moment of truth, sat in the Clickety-Clack moment and found the courage to be deeply honest with who I was.

How did you navigate the Clickety-Clack?

In that moment of hard truth, the first step was honesty. I gave myself permission to listen to the depths and different layers of myself. I realized I was functioning primarily from my head. I was ticking all the boxes. I was successful in a good life, but each time I started my car, I was driving in that same lane. I *wanted* to change lanes, change lanes in my own life.

I had to do a real assessment of what was and was not in alignment with who I was, not so much about what was and was not working.

I had to come back into myself, finding:

- My own depth
- How to understand myself
- What my best life was going to be
- Why I was not on a path to my best life
- Why I was on my current road
- Why I felt the pull and calling to change lanes

I started connecting with myself in lots of different ways. As I was studying in university, I explored ancient wisdom. I was embedded in the rational and science-based mind as well. I searched for ways to bridge those two beautiful sources of knowledge into a wisdom I could use to navigate my life into the lane I wanted to be in, that I felt called to be in, rather than the lane that looked good on the outside as a *good life*.

I began walking back into the calling I had felt all my life. I started to understand myself and my life as an ecosystem. I could not function just from my head anymore; I had to anchor and listen to my heart, my intuition, and my deeper knowing.

I needed to listen to my body, as well, because I had always pushed it.

I spent a lot of time journaling and writing. I was trying to understand the difference I sought. I gave myself permission to live a good life—the great life I was called toward.

What tools do you recommend for staying peaceful in a seemingly toxic world?

I listen to my head, my heart, my intuition—or my deeper knowing—and my body. I don't only listen to those components; I listen to them talk to each other as well. I start every day with a check-in, a meditation, and a bit of a scan. I ask each one of these areas—head, heart, intuition, and body—where they are and what that they need me to know for the day. I also decide how I would like to feel at the end of the day. I check in every morning.

Opening communication within myself allows me always to be in tune with my life as an ecosystem, an organic and fluid motion. When I am aware and always tuned in to all those layers within myself, I allow them to help me navigate my moments and my choices. Ultimately, this process helps me stay in that great life lane because I am more myself in everything I do. I experience the outside world and my inner landscape with such greater depth, beauty, and connection that it builds a great life; it builds a richness in my world, regardless of what is going on.

Whether I am joyful, a bit out of alignment, or dealing with something I have no control over, my way of relating to each situation changes. I take the wisdom of all those layers and learn. I create wisdom from those sources rather than simply acknowledging them. Together, it all builds experiences and creates a wisdom I then take back into my life ecosystem.

I seek the wisdom of nature as well. Always tune and connect by spending time in nature. See the great teacher she is when you gaze deeply into nature, how she functions and what she does. She is such an example to our personal ecosystem. I draw a lot of wisdom from spending time watching and being in natural spaces, and you can as well.

It is not just about building knowledge in your life; it is about building the wisdom that is an interconnection between those knowledge-building blocks and your attunement with your unique self. When you combine those two things, you can be in the world in your best life.

About the Author

Dr. Cassie Schwind has been in the field of psychology for twenty years. In her work, she found a common theme: Women were losing their sense of self as they collected roles and expectations during their life. Dr. Cassie traveled across the world and explored ancient wisdoms and soul-based coaching and broadened her work as a women's passion and purpose coach. She shows women who are disillusioned and dissatisfied with life to re-find their unique seed and re-landscape their life in order to thrive. She teaches women to reconnect their inner and outer landscapes to be more aligned as the women they know themselves to be.

She believes *all* women are leaders. She wants all women to *live fully*, *lead passionately*, and *love boldly* in work and in life.

You can find out more about Dr. Cassie's Self Embodied Living™ and Self Embodied Woman™ programs or get her free downloads *Stop Impostering* or *Don't Let Busy Be Your Buzz* at drcassie.net.

Jennifer Sprague

How has the Clickety-Clack shown up in your life?

The Clickety-Clack showed up in my life when I realized it was time to switch careers. I spent fifteen years in a career that I tried to make work. I was a high school teacher. I thought it was a gift to be a teacher and that I should be satisfied, happy, and content. However, I experienced overwhelming stress and anxiety about doing my best job and all the to-do items that seemingly never ended.

The stress led to health problems. I spent ten years trying to figure out where those health problems came from, but in the end, I received some guidance from a mentor. She basically gave me permission to quit. That was the best day of my life, so far, and that was when the Clickety-Clack began. When I finally had the courage to make that one decision, things started to align in my life.

I had always been a seeker, a spiritual person, and the reason I had not quit was because I could not see what to do next. I had no idea. I did not know what I would be doing if I were not a teacher, so I stayed. When I decided to quit, I did not know what I was going to do, but within two weeks, another friend suggested this thing called *coaching*. I had never heard of it.

I was considering earning another degree and spending money to go back to school, but when I researched coaching, I thought: *Holy cow! I am made for that.* I have always been a health and self-improvement junkie, especially in my choice of books. My mom would always try to get me to read fiction books, but I wouldn't.

I looked into coaching, and the day I looked, I signed up. From that point on, everything was exciting, and I felt like I was on the right path. I felt supported. As I moved out of a teaching career, all the details on the path easily fell into place. I sold my home, so I had some money to relocate and start my business.

Now, every time I stabilize in a position and feel content, there is a new opportunity for another Clickety-Clack moment. When I feel that, it's time to level up and move to the next stage of my own learning and development.

How did you navigate the Clickety-Clack?

This is where I got to put all the tools I have learned from self-help books into practice. Coming from the world of teaching, the best and hardest tool for me to practice was being present in the moment. That moment of presence is where I received guidance about my next action step or the next inspired idea. I continually came up against my past pattern of filling my time by saying yes to everything and trying to prove I was worthy of any financial compensation I was receiving. I was reliving the patterns I'd developed as a teacher.

It was a huge task to interrupt my pattern of doing, doing, doing and find more time to be, so that I could allow the steps to present themselves without me forcing so much. The first thing that needed to happen was for me to pause and be present in the moment. Next, I practiced continuous self-reflection and self-awareness, noticing every time I was in that mode of anxiety and trying to do too much to prove my worthiness or ability.

When I was not able to interrupt the old patterns, I sought support. This was a huge step for me, and I like to share it in my coaching. We are not meant to change on our own; we are social beings. Seeking guidance from teachers, authors, YouTube, inspiring webinars, and coaching practices was crucial for me to be able to interrupt my patterns and create the space in my life to allow synchronicities to flow in.

Synchronicities are happening all the time, whether or not I am present enough to see them or trust and have faith enough to take action. In fact, faith and trust are my last pieces. I do not need to know the full picture; I need to keep moving toward what I desire, trusting the next step will present itself. If I take action, the next step *will* present itself. The less I resist and try to think my way through things, the easier those synchronicities seem to flow into my life, and the more fun it becomes.

What tools do you recommend for staying peaceful in a seemingly toxic world?

The most effective strategy for me, and yet the simplest, is to stop and breathe more deeply. I love yoga. I have been a student of yoga and its philosophy for years, and I went through yoga instructor training so I could learn more about it.

It has taken me years to be able to pause and breathe deeply. In those moments when I can breathe deeply and have that connection with what I call my Higher Self, the natural question is always: *What do I really want?* I need to ask regularly. To stay peaceful in a seemingly toxic world starts with finding the peaceful moment by returning to my breath and asking what I really want—not what the world wants from me, what my loved ones want, or what my work expects from me.

What do I really want?

I have faith and trust that what I really want is what is best for my loved ones, for my work, and for the world. That peaceful experience is crucial because it maintains my energy frequency. If I am in an anxious or fearful energy state, then I am not going to be open to my Higher Self and the guidance it shows me. I pause to cultivate peace so I can reconnect with what I want, and it always revolves around feeling good.

As a coach, the main thing I do is help people develop self-care practices. That is the key to fulfilling your purpose—to take care of yourself. It always begins with slowing down so that you can leave space to find out what you want. When you are in that slower state, breathing deeply, feeling embodied and present, then it becomes clear what you really want, and you can take a baby step toward that desire without feeling any fear or any guilt. Have complete confidence in your Higher Self and the Universe to guide you there.

The purpose of slowing down is to cultivate awareness in your everyday moments. The more aware you become, the more the synchronicities can flow into your life, and you can see them. Those synchronicities are the crucial aspects of navigating the seemingly toxic world and maintaining your own high energy, emotions, and feelings.

The purpose of maintaining those high frequency energies, feelings, and emotions is to align with our purpose, and I think that is why we are all here.

About the Author

Jennifer Sprague enthusiastically and passionately guides clients and young adults toward their best selves through habit and lifestyle change. This inevitably includes developing self-awareness, building resilience, discovering passions, and aligning with purpose. She is the transformational health coach of Best Self with Jen Sprague, LLC, a certified yoga instructor, and an animal lover on the side.

Jennifer earned a bachelor's degree in biology and a master's in the art of teaching degree. She taught high school science for fifteen years prior to coaching, and she's thrilled to recently add young adults to her coaching roster—a true gift to support our next generation.

If you're not feeling great in your body or in your life, reach out for support; having experienced chronic health issues from years of stress and anxiety, she's been there and knows the way out. It's time we reclaimed our Best Selves.

If you're ready for support in slowing down so you can be present for the synchronicities and align with your purpose, visit her website, JenSprague.com. You can schedule a complimentary discovery session and sign up for her newsletter to receive a free guide to Cultivating Awareness.

Linda Tan

How has the Clickety-Clack shown up in your life?

The Clickety-Clack has shown up in my life since the COVID lockdown. It's hard to stay home when you are a businessperson who is used to being outside all the time. That has affected me a lot. My sister passed away in June of 2019, and my mother passed away in February of 2020. That certainly affected my life, and that was before the pandemic.

This disease has brought my life down a little bit. I have not had COVID, but I have been around people who have. My family is private, so it is hard to meet with them. Currently, they do not want to see me in person. They want to see me by Zoom, and it is hard to live life alone.

Business has been very, very quiet. Most of my business is done internationally; we create jewelry talismans and good luck jewelry, and we do it with stones. We bless them spiritually so that each person who wears one has their best life. I wanted everybody to understand that our jewelry and talismans are good omens. You can use them for prayer and for sicknesses.

A talisman is like a charm; you can wear one on your hand like a bracelet, or you can wear it as a necklace. They are designed in brilliant colors and are beautiful. I wear one all the time because it brings me peace and joy at this time that is so difficult.

Being stuck at home has impacted my life a lot, but our jewelry makes me happy and joyful and has helped me be more positive. My business is better overall than a lot of people's who have had to close.

How did you navigate the Clickety-Clack?

I do meditation every day. I joined the Christy Whitman program, and I learn from her experiences. I listen to parts of her program, which centers me. It has given me an understanding of where I am going and what I am doing. I am learning to love myself for who I am. I've learned to enjoy life whether it's with very little or with everything. I bring all this wealth, not just money, to my decision making, and I look toward what is coming.

I trust that everything I think about I also make happen in the most positive ways for myself. I have been with Christy Whitman for three years, and I have changed my whole understanding of what I was born for, where I am going, and what will make me happy. I love all the people I have met through her teachings. Everybody is so positive. They accept each person as a human with all these spiritual and glorious experiences, manifesting where they are going and loving every minute of it.

Right now in Columbia, I am enjoying the colors, the rain, the forest, the butterflies, the lizards, the roosters—everything is so beautiful, and it is such a joy.

What tools do you recommend for staying peaceful in a seemingly toxic world?

One tool that I recommend is to meditate every day. The meditation does not have to be for a long time; it could be for three seconds, one minute, or twenty minutes. I have an alarm on my telephone, and every hour and ten minutes, I hear it. I stop and come to a place of gratitude. I thank whatever I am doing, blessing it to make it better. I always bring my angels and everybody who has helped me. I bring them into my mind as soon as I hear the alarm.

Every time I do not like something, I click it away and turn to what I want to do. As soon as I am doing what I really want to do, I feel comfortable, not negative. I've been training my body not to have any pain. I see the space and wonder of the world and focus on having all the wealth I want.

You need to gain understanding of why you do things the way you do and how your parents or your experiences have influenced what you think. Pay attention to what you eat and all the vices you have. Many negative feelings and habits were taught to you as a child. Everything comes from your experiences, even though you may not realize what you have until you use tools to bring them to your awareness.

I see prosperity as I had not seen it before. For example, I look at a gemstone and see the multiple colors, all the facets that work together to bring you prosperity. I see the beauty of my business and of everybody I do business with. I work to understand what they are saying to me. When we truly see each other, it is such a wonderful, wonderful feeling.

These tools will bring you what you want for your business, which is love and understanding for each person, knowing what they want is good for them. That is such a beautiful, beautiful feeling. I love every minute of it!

My alarm reminds me to remember and focus on these positive things. It helps me remember to turn away from the Clickety-Clack.

About the Author

Linda Tan is a spiritual entrepreneur who has been in this business for four years. Her company, Four Points, LLC, specializes in talismans, which are a blend of different metals. Depending on a person's own spiritual needs, lucky charms are created for each individual. They are handmade and add spiritual protection to safeguard the wearer. This unique jewelry channels gifts of magnetic energy. Prepared under the constellation of the individual buyer, each piece attracts love and wards off evil. They also channel good energy and magnetize abundance.

Linda loves to help and serve humanity with her talismans (lucky charms).

To learn more about Linda's talismans, email: Lindafourpoints@gmail.com.

Tel# 619-882-0770

Joe Vitale

How has the Clickety-Clack shown up in your life?

Let me be blunt and transparent. The last two years have been the worst of my entire life, and my life has included homelessness and poverty. I am age sixty-seven. The last two years began with a divorce, a divorce I thought would be easy, effortless, maybe even have some joy in it because I was offering the moon to take care of my soon-to-be ex. Instead, it was a two-year persecution of my life and business with a woman full of rage and poison, directed at me.

I was shocked. The situation was difficult to accept and deal with, but I dealt with it on a daily basis, never knowing it would last two years. During the same two years, I developed a relationship with a new partner who contracted Lyme disease. Her Lyme disease was neurological; she could not drive, and she had trouble thinking and performing some normal tasks. I became her caregiver. This was during the divorce.

Also, my father died. On one level, his death was expected, as he was ninety-three. It was still a shock to the system. It not only shocked me, but one of my family members attempted suicide right after our loss. Then, my best friend died.

Of course, we all share the experience of this pandemic. The pandemic basically wiped out my biggest livelihood; my speaking engagements and my big pay from being on stage was brought to zero.

So, the last two years have been a Clickety-Clack ride to hell.

How did you navigate the Clickety-Clack?

How *are* you navigating the Clickety-Clack is the correct way to phrase it, because I am not done. The divorce is almost completed. We are nearing the end of it, but it is still going on because of a lack of forgiveness and understanding, maybe on everybody's part. I have had to go to urgent care a couple of times because of my stress levels, so I am not afraid to ask for help.

Navigating the Clickety-Clack should not be a lone-ranger, solitary experience. It is tough enough to go through these curve balls from life all by yourself, so seeking support is a big one. Going to urgent care is highly unusual in my life because I am healthy. But when I needed it, I was glad it was there.

I have also used traditional counseling. I have gone to healers and to people who practice different modalities. Of course, I know the different tools I have taught in my own life. There is *Ho'oponopono*, the Hawaiian healing technique I have written about in three books at this point, *Zero Limits*, *At Zero*, and the newest, *Fifth Phrase*.

I practice EFT, the Emotional Freedom Technique. I learned it way back when it was called TFT, Thought Field Therapy, invented by Roger Callahan.

I also have gleaned a lot from stoicism. Because of my research into and study of stoicism, I would call it a way to be an empowered victim. In other words, I still am going through and navigating this Clickety-Clack we call life, but I am doing it with an awareness that I have the ability to handle myself. If you can handle your mindset, you can handle your emotions.

The poster boy for stoicism, Marcus Aurelius, the ancient emperor of Rome, said, "If you can endure it, then endure it. Stop complaining."

Quotes like that end up on the wall behind me because they carry me through the day. Another phrase I often use is:

> *One day at a time, is all fine.*
> *One day at a time, is all fine.*
> *One day at a time, is all fine.*

What tools do you recommend for staying peaceful in a seemingly toxic world?

The first tool is the tool of choice: Disconnect from the toxicity. People are watching the mainstream news. The mainstream news is designed to program its watchers to fear. It is not going to assist you in surviving or thriving beyond the Clickety-Clack experience. The power of choice means turning off the news. You can choose to do that. Stay away from anything that is toxic in your life, which can be people, groups, the media, or even the government. Turn it off; turn a deaf ear to it.

Practice a couple of things I mentioned: EFT, which is the Emotional Freedom Technique, the tapping cure. There are plenty of books out there about that. Practice Ho'oponopono. I have written books on it, but there are other materials and videos available as well.

I am a great believer in seeking support. Create a mastermind group. Being in the right groups will support you. Supporting other people is also a way to support yourself.

Watch your mindset. You can choose what you are reading, what you are watching, what you are listening to. Your mindset is controlled by you, even though it may not feel like it at times.

Another take-away is that you are not your mind. You are not your brain. You are separate from your mind. You are separate from your brain. With that knowledge and wisdom, you have the ability to choose how you operate your mind and brain. So, I say choose the positive. Look for the good. Practice gratitude, as that is one of the most impactful things we can all do. In any time, any place, anyone can find something to be grateful for that can transform their life forever.

About the Author

Dr. Joe Vitale is the author of far too many books to mention here. Here are just a few of them:

He wrote the bestseller, *The Attractor Factor: 5 Easy Steps for Creating Wealth (or Anything Else) From the Inside Out*. It became a number-one bestseller twice, even beating the contemporary Harry Potter book.

He also wrote *Life's Missing Instruction Manual: The Guidebook You Should Have Been Given at Birth*. It, too, became a number-one bestseller and was picked up by Walmart.

One of his most popular titles, *Zero Limits: The Secret Hawaiian System for Wealth, Health, Peace, and More* reflects the ancient Hawaiian practice, Ho'oponopono. A fan favorite, Joe has hosted multiple live events on the subject nationwide, and he has created quite a following for this title alone.

To learn more about Dr. Vitale, visit: MrFire.com.

Lisa Warner

How has the Clickety-Clack shown up in your life?

The Clickety-Clack showed up in my life in the form of cancer. When I was a little girl, I had some profound experiences people would probably call mystical, but I simply called them *awareness*. I knew the history of humanity. I could see that humans were fighting with each other over money and land and over whose God was better. I was able to see overriding patterns of human mis-creations that had been repeating themselves through history when I was falling asleep at night.

I could look at the Earth from a distance, almost like floating in space. It was not that I was looking at the Earth; I was looking at the history of humanity, and I could see the wars. I could see people in nursing homes who could no longer take care of themselves because their bodies and their minds were no longer functioning properly.

As a child, I knew that was not right. I knew that was not the way it needed to be. I knew something different was possible. I knew we were designed to live in perfectly healthy bodies for a long time, and that I was meant to live in a perfectly healthy body for a long time. I knew I was meant to live for 150 or 200 years. It was clear to me.

However, when I looked around on this planet, I did not see that reality. I saw humanity struggling. I saw that humans were asleep. We are body, mind, and soul. The soul is the infinite part of us, the part that does not die, the part that exists forever. I saw that humanity had forgotten that we are the soul, and I saw that humans were operating just from their minds. I saw that, throughout history, the humans who had remembered their soul and are unconditional love they were healers who had come to help humanity. Somehow, however, that always went wrong, and they were the ones being strung up on crosses, burned at the stake, or beheaded.

As a child, I had that same awareness and those options did not really seem palatable to me, so I shut down my awarenesses because I did not feel safe. It was not safe to know that I was the infinite soul because nobody else on the planet seemed to remember that. So I began operating from my mind with human rules rather than from the rules of the infinite Universe.

How did you navigate the Clickety-Clack?

The part of myself I had shut down as a child always seemed to be missing from my life. Life was rolling along, but it was like riding a bike uphill and in low gear. I never felt connected, and I could not figure out my role on this planet. I was always struggling. I was struggling with money; I was struggling with all kinds of things, including the right livelihood.

I had grown up as a healthy, fit athlete, and I was an accomplished figure skater. I had a body that could do anything, so I could always trust it. My body had my back! As I struggled with my life, my body stopped being healthy and fit. My body went from being slender, strong, and flexible to gaining weight and not feeling well. It became inflexible; it started having aches and pains. The more I struggled with my life, the more I struggled with my body, and the more I struggled with my body, the worst I felt about myself.

Finally, I found myself facing cancer. There it was, staring me in the face. None of the medical options for treatment resonated with me, so I realized I needed to heal myself. I needed to go back to my original awareness I had as a child, knowing that our bodies are meant to live healthy and fit for hundreds of years.

Instead of taking the traditional medical route, I chose to answer my wakeup call instead. It was time for me to go back to knowing what I knew as a child. I decided to learn how to heal myself because I knew this was my call to mastery. I started to be quiet and tune in.

This cancer did not belong in my reality, so I knew I could change it. I knew that our bodies are designed to heal themselves because if we break a bone, sprain an ankle, or suffer a cut or bruise, our bodies automatically heal. I knew my body had the ability to heal itself, so I decided to trust my body. I started meditating, and I asked for inner guidance. One day in my mediation, I had a vision and knew automatically, right then and there, that cancer was not what was happening to my body or anybody else's body.

What tools do you recommend for staying peaceful in a seemingly toxic world?

The first tool I suggest is meditation because when we quiet the mind, we can receive extreme clarity. The clarity I received in my vision that day showed me that what we believe to be cancer and disease is actually not what is happening to our bodies. My body was out of balance because I was out of balance, and I suddenly understood that nothing was attacking my body. My body was simply sending me a message, but I had not been listening.

Once I became quiet and tuned in, I listened to my body and received the messages it was sending. I received the message that my body had my back. My body was on my side, my body wanted to live, my body wanted to heal itself. But, my body wanted me to get out of the way. My body wanted me to quiet my mind, to stop thinking and trying to figure things out.

My body needed me to be in my heart. My body needed me to be who I truly am: my higher self, the soul, the infinite self. I listened to my inner guidance. When our bodies feel good, our inner guidance is saying: *Yes, that is the right direction. Go for it! You are thinking the right thoughts. You are moving in the right direction.*

When we feel resistance in our bodies, feeling tension or closed off, our inner guidance system is saying: *No, that is not the right way to go. You are not thinking thoughts that are in alignment.*

When we are quiet, we can listen to our own inner guidance, and that inner guidance system always sends us in the right direction. It is always pointing us toward home, toward our self, toward our soul. It is always pointing us toward the unconditional love we are and toward the infinite well-being that is ours by nature. When we learn to trust our inner guidance, tune out the external world, and start tuning in to our own internal truth, that is when everything comes back into alignment.

That is when the Clickety-Clack goes away, and we can live our highest and best reality as our highest and best selves. I wrote the book, *The Simplicity of Self-Healing*, to help people start to change the way they perceive their bodies, to help them free themselves from the medical mindset of diseased-based thinking that is slowly killing us. We are infinite Beings, and we have the ability to create the healthy, wealthy, wise, and happy lives we desire—when we utilize the wisdom of our soul.

About the Author

Health innovator Lisa Warner always had the innate ability to perceive the world much more holistically than most, a gift which has helped deepen her conscious awareness of humanity's inner connection to Source. Even so, the realization she was facing cancer terrified her initially. The resulting experience, however, discovering her *SOULution* within, has been the catalyst for her remarkable work today as a sought-after speaker, facilitator, and author of *The Simplicity of Self-Healing*.

Lisa is passionate about showing us who we truly are, a perfect combination of mind, body, and soul divinely designed to be free of dis-ease. Once we transcend the limited mental programming of the *medical mindset*, we realize that our body is functioning flawlessly. What we perceive as a health issue is actually the body's response to unresolved emotional conflict. It's all about shifting our perspective. As the embodied connection to Source, *we* have all the power.

Visit ConnectingYoutoYou.com to find out more about Lisa and what she has to offer, including her six-week program, *Conscious*

Self Healing. This groundbreaking program shows how amazing our bodies are while simultaneously helping participants step into their higher power, creating desired health and well-being. Her book, *The Simplicity of Self-Healing*, is available here: bit.ly/ TheSimplicityofSelfHealing.

$\mathcal{L}$eslie $\mathcal{W}$arren

How has the Clickety-Clack shown up in your life?

The Clickety-Clack has shown up in my life in a lot of different ways. Most recently, it showed up in my broken body. I am a fitness trainer, a personal trainer. I use my body every day, all day, in what I do and how I help people. My body broke down, which led to having medical procedures to bring my body back to working and optimal shape.

The Clickety-Clack has shown up as me feeling isolated and depressed. In my work as a trainer, I have usually come up with great ideas and wonderful content I wanted to create and get out to the world to help people while recovering. That process has fallen flat. I have great ideas, and yet, nothing happens; I don't take action to move those ideas out of my head and into the world in some sort of beneficial content creation. The content simply does not get created.

First, it has been difficult for my body not to work because it is primarily how I express myself and contribute to the world. Second, it is hard to have a great idea, something I want to contribute and start, only to then have it fall flat through inaction. These two things have come to a head, and I feel depressed and beat myself up because I know I can do better. In my heart, I know I can do it. Still, it does not happen, and that situation and feeling are not always pleasant.

How did you navigate the Clickety-Clack?

Personal development is not something you do once. It is an ongoing process to continually improve and become the best version of yourself, and it is what has allowed me to find ways to go *through* and process what is uncomfortable to get to that better version of me.

When there is uncomfortable stuff going on, you cannot go around it, you cannot go under it, you cannot over it. You must go through it and process it. In our culture, we have learned not to process and go through things but to endure the uncomfortableness. We run away from things that are uncomfortable. We always want to stay in the happy place, in the good-feeling place, and not face the ugly, the contrast, the hard stuff.

I have learned to navigate through the Clickety-Clack by looking it straight in the face, taking a deep breath, and taking one step toward it. I do not force myself to go through it; instead, I surrender because I know the best way to get through anything is to go through it by surrender instead of by resistance.

Do not try going around it. Do not try to dodge it. Do not try to put it off until later. Take a deep breath, release, and surrender to the fact that going through is the best way. Take a look in the mirror and face the parts of your situation/yourself you do not like, and face them with love. Look at yourself as you look at a baby because no one is going to yell at a little baby for the things they cannot do. You look at a small child with compassion and love. You need to look at yourself/your situation that same way.

I have reached out to people who are important to me, professionally and personally, and asked for their guidance. Some of these people I know personally, one-on-one. Some of them are people I do not know personally, but I access their information in books or in their webinars. I do not know Martin Luther King Jr., but I can read his biography. I do not know Oprah Winfrey, Lisa Nichols, or Vishen Lakhiani, but I can go to Mindvalley.com, the website Vishen created. I can reach Lisa Nichols and Oprah Winfrey through books. I receive help from mentors I know personally and from mentors I do not know.

What tools do you recommend for staying peaceful in a seemingly toxic world?

I believe in meditation. I had a hard time doing it in the past, but since then, I have realized there is no right way to do it. You just do it. I have used several tools that have helped me meditate. Some of them worked; some of them did not. I kept going until I found one that did work. I knew intuitively that meditation was going to be essential, so those failed attempts were not necessarily failures. They were simply steps in which I learned what methods did not work for me and which ones did. So, meditation has been important.

Recently, I have been using a program called *Alignment Essentials*. I have known about it since its creation. The founder, Jani Roberts, is one of my mentors, and using their different moving meditations has helped me through some of the difficult things I see in the mirror.

Finally, I remind myself that no matter what process I am going through in life, I have a choice. I am not a victim. I can choose to be a victim, or I can choose to be in charge and stand in my power. It took me a long time to understand that. I now fully realize that truth in my being and embrace it.

I breathe in this thinking deeply, so I can remember when I am not feeling good, that feeling good is not a circumstance. Feeling good is a choice. I keep reminding myself that even when I am feeling awful, I can make a different choice by taking time to surrender to whatever is going on. That does not mean I give up. I simply recognize that what is going on is not permanent. Even if it were permanent, I could face it and choose happiness, choose joy.

Keep choosing joy. Choosing happiness. Choosing love. Every moment. What you have is *now*, and *now* is eternal if you keep making the choice to go through life happily. As long as you choose joy and happiness, you will find they become your *now* all the time.

About the Author

Leslie Warren started her fitness career by accident. She had been invited for months by her mom to take a class called Zumba® Fitness and would not take it, at first. Little did she know or was she prepared for what happened in that first fateful class.

Fast-forward a decade, and Leslie teaches over ten formats—six of the Zumba® Fitness specialties, Alignment Essentials®, and Bootcamp; created two formats: Crazy 80s Cardio™ and K-Sera™; and is a trainer. She is a passionate and dedicated fitness professional, always improving and increasing her skill and knowledge-base in order to provide the best, most fun, and inspiring workout for her clients.

Leslie believes that anything is possible, and to that end, she is currently training for her first bodybuilding competition in 2021. Her fitness philosophy is: *If it isn't fun, let's make it fun!*

She's the proud mom of two boys and three fur babies.

Please go to ThePhoenixFitness.com for a free gift or join Leslie on Instagram @the.phoenix.fitness or on Facebook at The Phoenix Fitness.

Conclusion

As you reach the end of this book, our hope as the publisher is that you have been inspired by the incredible people we invited to share insights, stories, tips, and tools for navigating the Clickety-Clack of life and staying peaceful within, even when things around you are seemingly toxic.

You may have noticed we used the word *seemingly* in front of the word *toxic*. This is for a specific purpose. Many of our authors love the world and are able to accept whatever is happening around them, still seeing the world as good. Because they use the tools they shared with you, they are either unphased by outward appearances, or in many cases, the time they stay in the negative passes quickly. Seeing the world as toxic is ultimately a choice. One can look at the same event and see it as toxic, or a challenge, a learning experience, or, as some say, "It is what it is." It's all perspective.

As you read our authors' answers to the three questions, did you feel connected to any of them or their perspectives?

If you connected to any of our contributors in strong and meaningful ways, we suggest you reach out to them. Look up the people, websites, programs, or products they mentioned within their chapter of the book.

Our wish for you—like those we invited to be in this book—is to be a walking, talking demonstration of being able to stay neutral, calm, and peaceful no matter what is happening in the outside world.

Thank you for reading this book!

Keith Leon S.

5x International Award-Winning Author, Speaker, and Publisher

LeonSmithPublishing.com

BeyondBeliefPublishing.com

About the Publisher

In 2004, Babypie Publishing was founded by entrepreneurs Keith and Maura Leon when they decided to self-publish their co-authored book, *The Seven Steps to Successful Relationships.* When Babypie published its second book, Keith Leon's, *Who Do You Think You Are? Discover the Purpose of Your Life*, a few years later—implementing a large marketing campaign that introduced the book to over a million people on the first day it came out—both books became bestsellers overnight.

After the success of their first two titles, Keith and Maura were approached by another author who believed they could take his book to bestseller status as well. They decided to give it a shot, and Warren Henningsen's book, *If I Can You Can: Insights of an Average Man*, became an international bestseller the day it was released.

Before long, Babypie Publishing was receiving manuscript submissions from all over the world and publishing such titles as Ronny K. Prasad's, *Welcome to Your Life*; Melanie Eatherton's, *The 7-Minute Mirror*; and Maribel Jimenez and Keith Leon's,

The Bake Your Book Program: How to Finish Your Book Fast and Serve It Up HOT!

With a vision to make an even greater impact, Babypie Publishing began offering comprehensive writing and publishing programs, as well as a full range of à-la-carte services to support independent authors and innovative professionals in getting their message out in the most powerful and effective manner. In 2015, Keith and Maura developed the YouSpeakIt book program to make it easy, fast, and affordable for busy entrepreneurs and cutting-edge health practitioners to get their mission and message out to the world.

In 2016, Leon Smith Publishing was created as the new home for Babypie, YouSpeakIt, and future projects. In 2018, Beyond Belief Publishing was added as an imprint for spiritual and esoteric titles.

Whether you're a transformational author looking for writing and publishing services, or a visionary leader ready to take your life and work to the next level, we thank you for visiting our website at LeonSmithPublishing.com and look forward to serving you.

Made in the USA
Monee, IL
20 April 2021